how to install
PANELING
VALANCES·CORNICES
WALL-TO-WALL STORAGE
CEDAR ROOM·FIREPLACE MANTEL

Donald R. Brann

SEVENTEENTH PRINTING — 1979
REVISED EDITION

Published by
DIRECTIONS SIMPLIFIED, INC.

Division of
**EASI-BILD PATTERN CO., INC.
Briarcliff Manor, N.Y. 10510**

Library of Congress Card No. 65-25756

FIRST PRINTING
© 1960

REVISED EDITIONS
1962,1964,1965,1967,
1968,1969,1970,1971,
1972,1974,1975,1977
1979

NOTE:
All metric dimensions shown are within 5/100 of a centimeter.

Due to the variance in quality and availability of many materials and products, always follow directions a manufacturer and/or retailer offers. Unless products are used exactly as the manufacturer specifies, its warranty can be voided. While the author mentions certain products by trade name, no endorsement or end use guarantee is implied. In every case the author suggests end uses as specified by the manufacturer prior to publication.

Since manufacturers frequently change ingredients or formula and/or introduce new and improved products, or fail to distribute in certain areas, trade names are mentioned to help the reader zero in on products of comparable quality and end use.   The Publisher

ANYBODY CAN DO ANYTHING

Installing beautifully finished plywood panels is not difficult, nor does it require any skill or woodworking experience. Everyone who takes the time to read through this book and to follow the simplified directions can successfully panel one wall, or an entire room with professional results assured.

Successfully doing something you have never done before is life's way of building a better individual. The physical work stimulates the body while it relaxes the mind. Working with your hands builds self confidence, attracts admiration from family and friends.

Everything you do to improve your home increases its value. Every new activity develops your personality. The key to your future rests solely with you. You can be a doer or a sitter, a leader or a follower. Read through this book and see how it opens doors to new opportunities.

Give this book to those approaching retirement. Note how it sparks their imagination. People who follow our simplified directions soon discover they are a lot handier with tools than they presumed. Starting on a project for their own homes, they are soon doing the same job for others. Before they fully realize what is happening, they are launched on a new career.

This book is one of a series designed to help people help themselves. Each provides step-by-step directions that show how to do something few have ever done before.

Try and you will succeed.

Don R. Brann

TABLE OF CONTENTS

CONSIDER THESE FACTS

Most people get enthused contemplating doing something they have never done before. They get equally confused, confounded and discouraged when they try to follow unfamiliar words and procedures. To eliminate confusion and to clarify every step, each is illustrated. Read completely through this book before buying any paneling or moldings. Note each illustration and you will immediately discover - paneling and/or building wall to wall closets, valances and cornice boards is real easy.

Since each room presents a different combination of problems, directions cover many situations. Place a check-mark alongside each paragraph that helps solve your problem.

When a new ceiling is to be installed, do ceiling first. If a suspended ceiling,* with or without lighting panels, is to be installed, first rough in wiring. A suspended ceiling should be installed after walls have been paneled.

*Complete directions for installing a luminous ceiling are explained in Book #694 Electrical Repairs Simplified.

7

Always butt panels together over a furring strip or stud. Furring strips are used to provide a plumb surface and firm base. If existing wall is plumb, plaster or existing wallboard firm, panels can be fastened with adhesive, or nailed over existing wall, no furring is required.

Consider any structural changes you would like to make. Do you need to build or remove a partition, closet, relocate a door, install wall outlets? Do it before paneling.

TOOLS NEEDED

You will need a hammer, crosscut and coping saw, plane, square, chalk line, plumb bob line, level, nailset, folding rule and screw driver, Illus. 1.

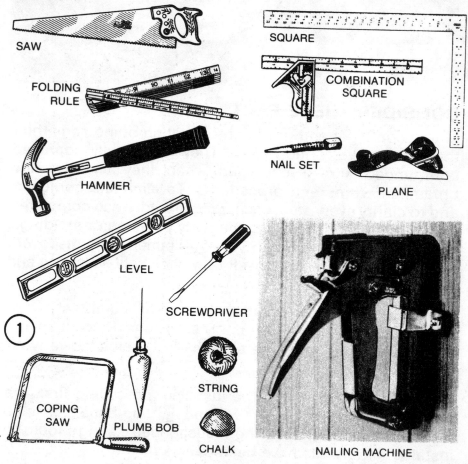

SAW

SQUARE

FOLDING RULE

COMBINATION SQUARE

HAMMER

NAIL SET

PLANE

LEVEL

SCREWDRIVER

1

COPING SAW

PLUMB BOB

STRING

CHALK

NAILING MACHINE

8

IT'S EASY WHEN YOU KNOW HOW

The first step in paneling a room is to decide what walls you want to panel. Since paneling adds to the value of your house, buy the best you can afford. You can usually recoup your entire investment when you sell. Next decide whether you want to panel from top of baseboard to ceiling, Illus. 2; butt panels against existing window and door casings, or would you prefer removing casings and applying matching trim. Many pros remove the shoe, baseboard and ceiling molding, then install paneling so it butts against existing door and window casings.

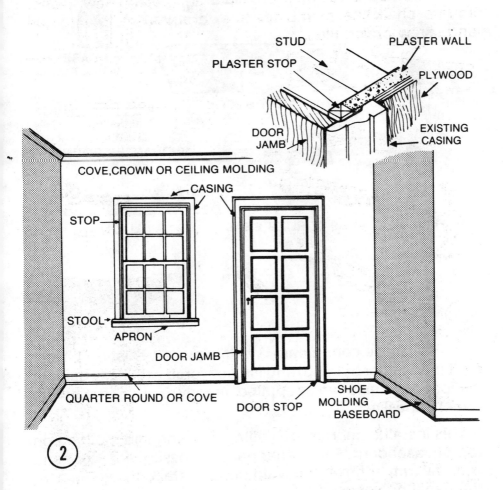

STUD

PLASTER WALL

PLASTER STOP

PLYWOOD

DOOR JAMB

EXISTING CASING

COVE, CROWN OR CEILING MOLDING

CASING

STOP

STOOL

APRON

DOOR JAMB

QUARTER ROUND OR COVE

DOOR STOP

SHOE MOLDING

BASEBOARD

2

To do a complete paneling job, the shoe, baseboard, ceiling molding, window and door casings are removed, new matching trim is applied, Illus. 3.

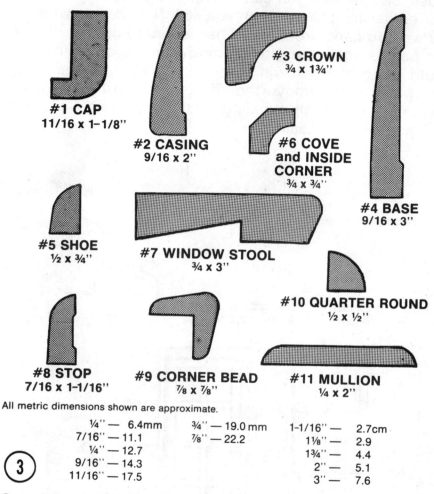

#1 CAP
11/16 x 1-1/8"

#2 CASING
9/16 x 2"

#3 CROWN
¾ x 1¾"

#6 COVE and INSIDE CORNER
¾ x ¾"

#4 BASE
9/16 x 3"

#5 SHOE
½ x ¾"

#7 WINDOW STOOL
¾ x 3"

#10 QUARTER ROUND
½ x ½"

#8 STOP
7/16 x 1-1/16"

#9 CORNER BEAD
⅞ x ⅞"

#11 MULLION
¼ x 2"

All metric dimensions shown are approximate.

¼" — 6.4mm	¾" — 19.0 mm	1-1/16" — 2.7cm
7/16" — 11.1	⅞" — 22.2	1⅛" — 2.9
¼" — 12.7		1¾" — 4.4
9/16" — 14.3		2" — 5.1
11/16" — 17.5		3" — 7.6

(3)

Consider these conditions. If wall is plumb, existing plaster isn't cracked or bulging, and isn't covered with flaky paint or wallpaper; panels can be applied directly to existing wall with panel adhesive.

In this installation, remove ceiling molding and molding on top of baseboard. Sandpaper paint off baseboard, door and window trim, refinish trim with antique stain to complement the paneling selected.

An easier, quicker and more professional way is to remove shoe and ceiling molding, baseboard, door and window casings, apply panels, then apply new trim, Illus. 4.

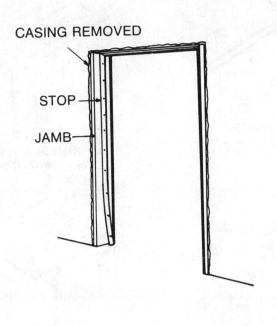

CASING REMOVED

STOP

JAMB

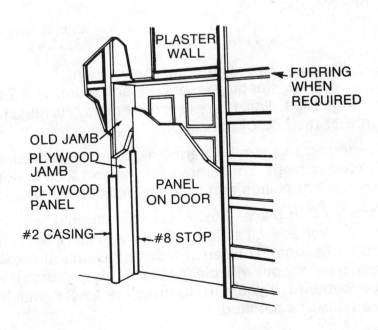

PLASTER WALL

FURRING WHEN REQUIRED

OLD JAMB

PLYWOOD JAMB

PLYWOOD PANEL

PANEL ON DOOR

#2 CASING

#8 STOP

(4)

If paint on wall is flaky or wallpapered, but still plumb, panels can be applied with matching colored nails, or veneer covered aluminum moldings, Illus. 5.

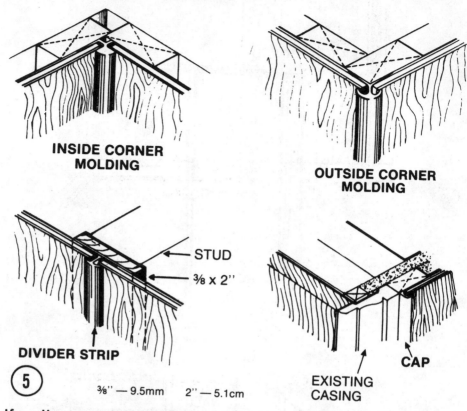

INSIDE CORNER MOLDING

OUTSIDE CORNER MOLDING

STUD

⅜ x 2"

DIVIDER STRIP

CAP

EXISTING CASING

(5) ⅜" — 9.5mm 2" — 5.1cm

If walls are covered with a soft panelboard, loose or cracked plaster, or plaster bulges, or wall isn't plumb, 1 x 2 or ⅜ x 2" furring strips, Illus. 6, are recommended. Furring strips offer another method of paneling.

Furring strips permit covering existing baseboard, door and window casings. You remove ceiling and shoe molding, then nail 1 x 2 at ceiling and at top of baseboard, Illus. 6.

Tack 1 x 2 in place, Illus. 6. Using a straight length of 2 x 4 and a level, see if it's plumb. Be sure to test every 4 ft. across width of a room. You can now drive the nails all the way in, or shim the 1 x 2 out with pieces of shingle to plumb it with face of baseboard. If you have to drive the 1 x 2 in real tight, use two nails at each stud.

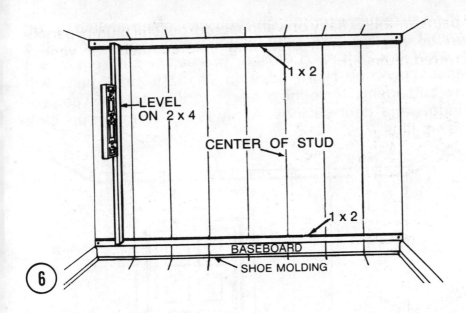

6

When the test pair of 1 x 2 are plumb, apply balance of furring strips, Illus. 7, 16" on centers horizontally, four feet on centers vertically.

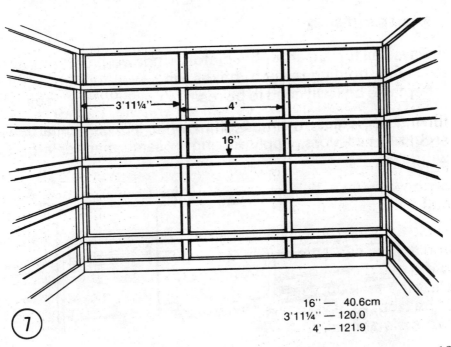

7

16" — 40.6cm
3'11¼" — 120.0
4' — 121.9

13

If the wall requires furring, and you want new paneling to butt against existing baseboard, window and door casings, use strips of ⅜ x 2" furring, Illus. 8. This can be cut from a 4 x 8 panel of plywood. Nail in position. The 3/16" or ¼" panel will now butt against top edge of baseboard, and against edge of window and door casings. Apply ⅜ x 2" strips in position shown, Illus. 7, 8.

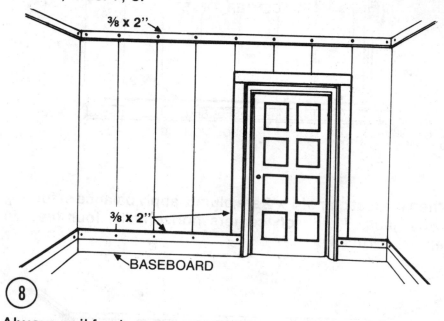

⅜ x 2"

⅜ x 2"

BASEBOARD

8

Always nail furring around radiator, windows, Illus. 9, 10, and to studs holding switch boxes and wall outlets. Each receptacle box will need to be reset to finish flush with panel.

Illus. 9 indicates furring strips nailed in position around recessed radiators. Apply furring in same manner around windows.

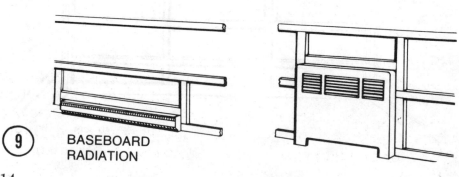

9 BASEBOARD
RADIATION

If paneling is being applied over existing plaster or gypsum board without furring, the screws holding switch or outlet can be loosened to permit outlet to finish flush with panel. In most cases, you don't have to reposition receptacle box.

When furring is required, outlet box should be reset as shown in Illus. 10. Paneling finishes flush with edge of box.

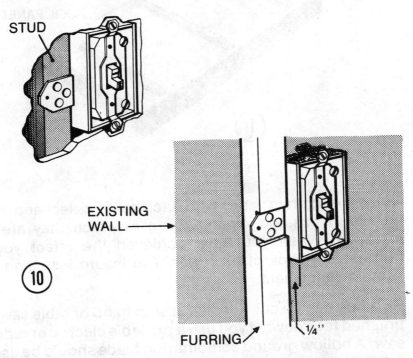

STUD

EXISTING WALL

(10)

FURRING

¼"

Another consideration that warrants an immediate decision is the question of adding more wall outlets, wall or ceiling lighting. It's a simple matter to cut an opening in existing wall, rough in wiring and install new outlets prior to paneling. Book #694 Electrical Repairs Simplified provides details.

There are other major improvements you may wish to consider before paneling. One is to divide a large room to make two. Another is to frame in a closet. Or move location of an interior door. While this requires paneling both sides of a wall, it frequently provides more usable wall space. Directions for building wall to wall closets start on page 40.

15

Place panels in the room they are to be installed. Separate panels with pieces of 1 x 2 to allow free flow of air to reach all panels, Illus. 11, for at least 48 hours.

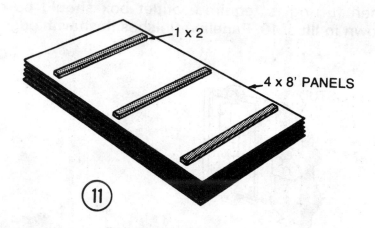

1 x 2

4 x 8' PANELS

(11)

Since wood grain varies with each panel, select and arrange panels in position around room in which they are to be installed. When you have achieved the effect you like, number the back of each panel to insure installing in the same arrangement.

Plywood can be cut with a crosscut hand or table saw. Keep finished face down if you use a portable electric or radial arm saw. A hollow ground combination blade should be used. Do not use a rip saw.

Use 3/16 or ¼" prefinished panels. These are available in 4 x 7 or 4 x 8 and in a wide variety of wood grains. When estimating number of panels a wall requires, always figure in windows and doors. Cutouts can be used to cover doors, make matching cabinets, etc.

To estimate number of panels required, measure the perimeter of a room and divide by four, Illus. 12. A 12 x 14' room = 12, 12, 14, 14, totals 52 ft. Divide by four equals 13 panels. Professionals frequently estimate 5% to 10% additional for waste.

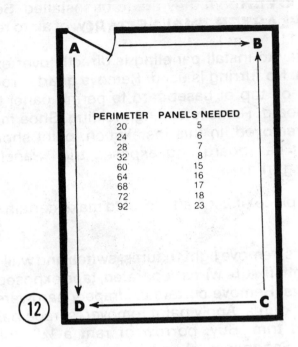

PERIMETER	PANELS NEEDED
20	5
24	6
28	7
32	8
60	15
64	16
68	17
72	18
92	23

_____4 x 7' (121.9 x 213.4cm)
_____4 x 8' (121.9 x 243.8cm)
_____3 x 10' (121.9 x 304.8cm)
_____1 x 2'' furring (2.54 x 5.1cm)
_____Panel Adhesive
_____Moldings as specified

Alway nail furring through existing wall covering into a stud. Wall studs are usually placed 16'' apart. To locate a stud, measure 16'' from a wall and test by driving a 6 penny nail into wall. Measure over 16'' to locate another. If you note where a baseboard was nailed, this usually indicates a stud.

Another way is to use a "magnetic stud locator." This zeros in on nails. When you locate one stud, measure same distance to locate others. Using a level, draw lines to indicate position of all studs. Continue lines one or two inches on ceiling and on floor, Illus. 6.

17

PANELING OVER
EXISTING PLASTER, WALLBOARD

The easiest way to install paneling is directly over existing walls, Illus. 13. No furring is used. Remove quarter round or cove molding on top of baseboard to permit panel to butt against baseboard. Remove ceiling molding. Shoe molding need not be removed. In this installation, paint should be removed from baseboard and exposed trim. Panels butt against existing trim.

Use a straight piece of 2 x 4 and level to make certain wall is plumb.

Switch off lights, remove light fixtures, switch and wall outlet plates. Keep light fixture wires separated, tape exposed ends or use wire nuts. Remove curtain or drapery hardware, and all projecting fixtures. Apply paint remover, scrape paint off baseboard and trim. Buy, borrow or rent a ¼" drill and sanding disc. Sandpaper all surfaces. Apply finish that matches panel.

Panel adhesive simplifies installing panels on any firm, smooth and plumb surface. It is stronger than nails, and sets fast. DO NOT USE on loose paint, loose wallpaper, over cracked or flaky plaster.

Since a house settles, lumber shrinks and warps, you seldom find a corner square, floor or ceiling level throughout a room. For this reason, always measure distance from ceiling to top of baseboard at corner and again four feet from same corner. Do the same at other end of each wall. Cut panel ¼" less than overall height.

Butt panel snugly in corner, Illus. 13. With level held on outside edge, check to make certain panel is plumb. The ¼" allowance should permit positioning panel plumb.* Fasten panel plumb with a couple of nails. Nails butt against edge of panel, not through panel. Or use two pieces of shingle as wedges, Illus. 14.

18   *NOTE: If corner is more than slightly out of plumb, it may be necessary to cut panel ⅜" less than overall height.

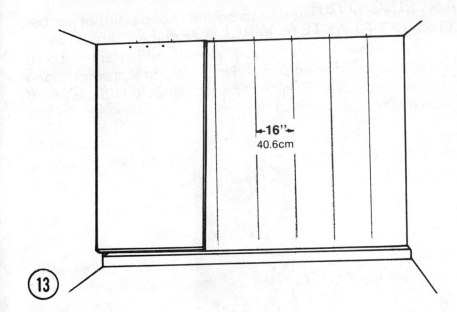

13

←16"→
40.6cm

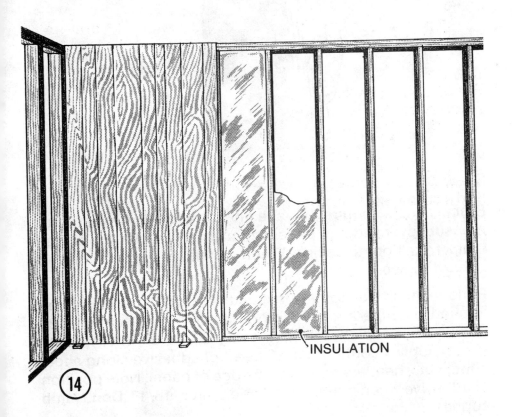

14

INSULATION

19

When panel is plumb, scribe to corner. Keep point of scriber following corner, Illus. 15, pencil on panel. A charcoal white pencil (available in art supply stores) will mark without damaging a prefinished panel. Remove panel, saw or plane along scribed line. Replace panel. Check with level. If necessary, scribe panel to ceiling.

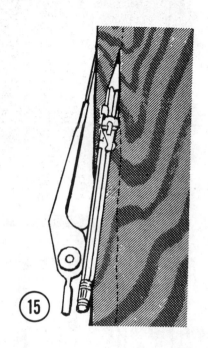

Since panels require ⅛" spacing to allow for expansion, measure over width of panel and paint a 1" wide strip of wall black from floor to ceiling. When panels are applied, the gap is hard to see.

Panel adhesive simplifies installation, but it should only be applied in temperatures ranging from 60° to 100°. Apply a 3" ribbon of ⅛" thick adhesive every 6", to all intermediate studs. Apply a continuous ⅛" bead of adhesive along shoe, plate, cats, headers and behind edge of panel. Note position of adhesive when butting two panels, Illus. 16, 17. Don't jamb edges.

Place panel back in position. Drive three 6 penny finishing nails about 8'' apart along top edge of panel, Illus. 13. This acts as a hinge. Press panel firmly in position, then pull out and block bottom edge 8 to 10'' from wall. This permits air to set adhesive until it gets tacky.

Remove blocks, press panel in position. Tap panel along stud lines with a rubber mallet or piece of 2 x 4 covered with carpet. Drive nails in at top, countersink heads, fill holes with matching Putty Stik.

When first panel is plumb, it simplifies installing other panels. Start at A and work toward B, Illus. 12, cutting last panel size to fit. Space panels ⅛'' apart. Start at C, work toward B and D. Fit each in position before applying adhesive. If panel is plumb, but doesn't butt squarely against ceiling or baseboard, you can get a tighter joint by beveling edge.

Always plan application so full panels butt together in the most prominent corner of the room. When panels have to be cut, butt cut panels together in the least conspicuous corner.

When applying panels over gypsum board, check the wallboard with a 4' level or straight edged 2 x 4 x 8'. Mark wall where you see any low spots. Cut first panel 32'' wide so edge of panel doesn't line up with edge of wallboard. Fill low spots with a heavier coating of adhesive.

21

APPLICATION OVER CRACKED PLASTER, LOOSE WALLPAPER, FLAKY PAINT

If existing wall requires furring, but you want to leave existing baseboard, window and door trim exposed, use ⅜ x 2" plywood furring, Illus. 8. Remove ceiling molding, cove or quarter round on top of baseboard. Measure 16" or distance required to locate a stud. Test to find one stud. Using a level, draw lines to indicate stud locations.

Nail ⅜ x 2" furring strips to studs with 8 penny common nails. With a straight 2 x 4 and a level, Illus. 6, check to make certain strips are plumb. If necessary, shim furring out with pieces of wood shingle. Use an extra 8 penny common nail at each stud to force furring in. When top and bottom strips are plumb, nail others in plumb position 16" apart, Illus. 7.

Toenail furring to window and door casing with 4 penny finishing nails.

Measure 3'11¼" and 4' and nail furring vertically to studs. If you can't nail into a stud, toenail to other furring. Follow procedure outlined for scribing and applying panels.

If you want paneling to cover a baseboard, remove shoe and ceiling molding. Nail a 1 x 2 at ceiling, another butting against top of baseboard. When plumb, nail other furring 16" apart. Nail 1 x 2 vertically in position shown.

If ceiling is greater than 8 feet, nail additional 1 x 2's required to support edge of panel.

Another way to apply paneling in a high ceiling room is with a chair rail. Cut bottom panels 30 to 36" high. Be sure to line up grooves and joints when butting top panels. Cover joint with #2 or #11 molding, Illus. 3.

If you want to remove baseboard, window and door casings and ceiling molding and apply panels over a firm wall, scribe panel to corner. Apply panel adhesive to drawn lines. Position panel plumb, Illus. 14. Follow adhesive manufacturer's directions when applying panels, Illus. 17.

22

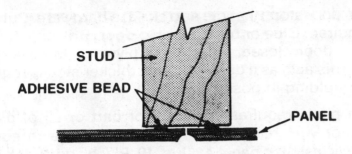

STUD

ADHESIVE BEAD

PANEL

(17) Paint exposed face of stud black or use black tape. Allow ⅛" between panels for expansion. Apply adhesive to stud, not to tape.

Should you prefer nailing panels, use 1" brads or 4 penny finishing nails. Nail outer edge of panel every 6", every 12" along stud lines, Illus. 18. A nailing gun, Illus. 1, speeds installation. If grooved paneling is being installed, nail panel as shown, Illus. 18. Avoid nailing in grooves. Always match groove over a stud.

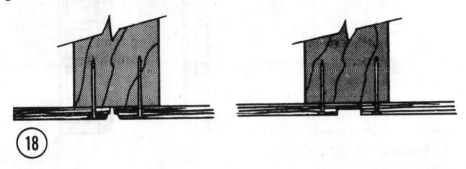

(18)

If V groove panels are being installed, drive nails in position shown. Use care to avoid damaging panel. Countersink heads with a nailset. Fill holes with Putty Stik.

If panel covers part or all of a window or door, place panel in position, mark outline of jamb on back of panel. Where it is not convenient to hold and mark back of panel, measure position of opening and mark same on panel, Illus. 4.

Illus. 19 shows panel being measured to cover part of opening. In each case the panel is wedged in plumb position before measuring size for cutout. Lines are then drawn on panel to exact size and position required. A saber saw permits cutting panel so cutout can be used to cover a door.

Remove door stops, handle and surface hardware. Cut panel size required. Glue or brad panel to door. Drill hole for door set. With door closed, cut strip of plywood to cover jamb, Illus. 4. This acts as a door stop. If a thicker stop is required, nail #8 molding in position.

When a panel requires a cutout for part or all of a door, window or wall receptacle, measure distance to edge of previously installed panel A, Illus. 19. Place and plumb panel in position A indicates. Using a level, draw lines to indicate opening.

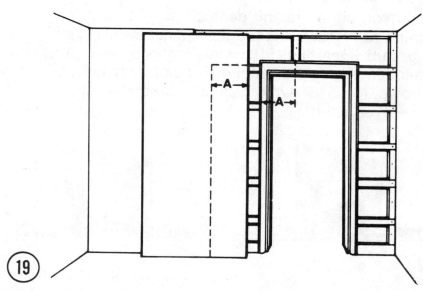

When a door or window is to be finished with new casings, the strip of paneling, cut to size jamb requires, Illus. 4, can be applied before or after wall paneling. The casing covers joint.

Another way to finish an exposed edge of a panel is with veneer faced aluminum cap molding, Illus. 5.

When a panel requires a cutout for an outlet box, plumb panel in position tight against ceiling. Draw top and bottom line of opening. Measure distance to edge of previously installed panel A, Illus. 20, 21. Carefully measure and cut opening for wall outlet. B, Illus. 21, represents distance from bottom of box to bottom of panel. C and D equal size of box.

24

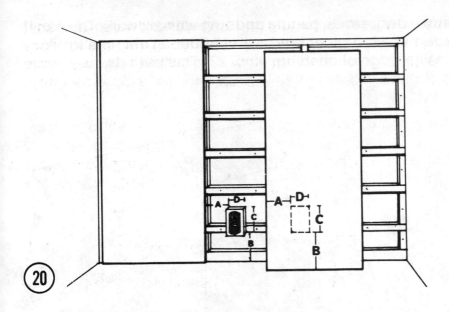

Drill ½" holes in position indicated. Use keyhole or saber saw to cut out for box.

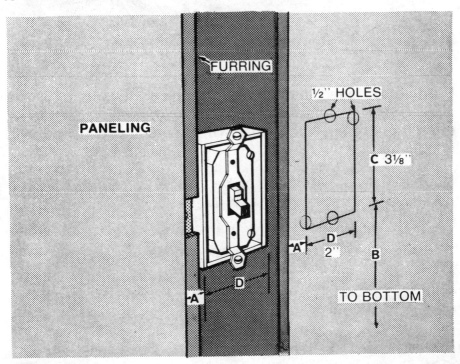

FURRING

PANELING

½" HOLES

C 3⅛"

D
2"

A

B

TO BOTTOM

½" — 12.7mm   2" — 5.1cm
3⅛" — 7.9

25

A saber saw permits cutting opening without drilling holes. If you don't have a saber saw, drill ⅛" holes at diagonal corners on inside edge of opening, Illus. 22. This permits inserting a keyhole saw.

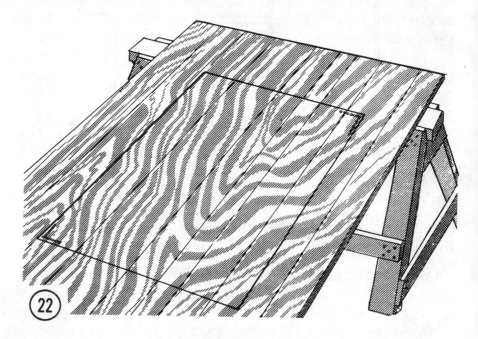

Hardwood faced aluminum moldings, Illus. 5, 23, are available in 8 ft. lengths. When used with prefinished panels, moldings should be finished with matching color prior to installation.

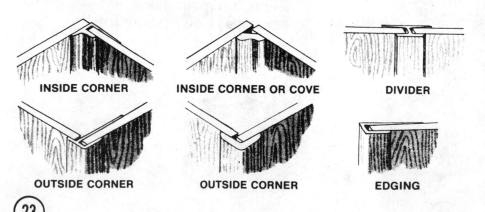

INSIDE CORNER   INSIDE CORNER OR COVE   DIVIDER

OUTSIDE CORNER   OUTSIDE CORNER   EDGING

To install, nail inside corner, Illus. 23, or cap in corner to a stud or furring strip. Be sure to plumb molding with level before nailing in place.

No vertical furring strips, Illus. 7, are required when using aluminum moldings. Butt edge of panel in corner molding, then pull it out ⅛" to allow for expansion. Nail panel every 16" with 1" brads along intermediate stud lines. Never use panel adhesive when installing panels with aluminum moldings. Cut divider to length required. Slip over edge of panel, check with level and nail divider in place.

Illus. 23 shows where veneer faced aluminum moldings are used.

Prefinished hardwood trim provides another easy way to apply paneling. The trim shown in Illus. 3, is available at building material dealers. Use #1 as an outside corner. Recess panel ¼" to allow nailing or gluing molding in position. Use #2 molding for door or window casing, also as a chair rail; #3 crown at ceiling; #4 at base; #5 shoe; #6 cove at ceiling or inside corner; #7 window stool; #8 stop; #9 outside corner; #11 as a mullion. This also can be used as a chair rail. Butt panels together, cover joint with #11. It can also be cut in half and used as window or door stop.

The top edge of panels in a high ceiling room can be finished with mullion #11. Cut one edge square, butt against panel. Paint or wallpaper can be applied above mullion .

Use #10 molding wherever ¼" quarter round is required. To avoid splitting, drill holes before nailing. Use 4 penny finishing nails.

When trimming a window or door, apply glue to all miter joints. Install door casing before installing base molding. Base molding butts against door casing.

If wall-to-wall carpeting is to be installed, butt carpet against paneling, no baseboard or shoe molding is installed.

If you decide to remove existing trim around a window, pry up and remove top casing, Illus. 24, then side casing. Remove stops. Hold sash in place with 6 penny nails. Remove apron. Knock up and remove stool. Cut a strip of paneling to size jamb requires, screw in place across top, then side of jamb. This now acts as a window stop.*

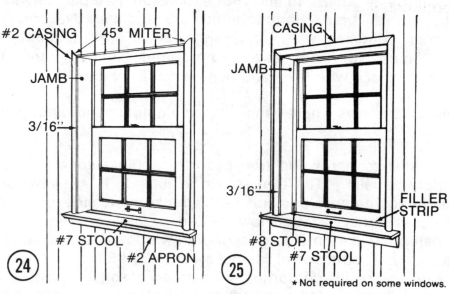

(24) #2 CASING — 45° MITER — JAMB — 3/16" — #7 STOOL — #2 APRON

(25) CASING — JAMB — 3/16" — FILLER STRIP — #8 STOP — #7 STOOL

* Not required on some windows.

Cut #7 prefinished hardwood window stool to width required. If 3" width of stool isn't wide enough, cut and nail a filler strip to width required, Illus. 25, 26. Stool should project over paneling 1".

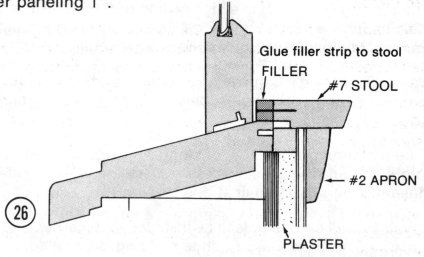

(26) Glue filler strip to stool — FILLER — #7 STOOL — #2 APRON — PLASTER

Temporarily hold stool in position with two blocks, Illus. 27. Check with level. With square, mark width of window on stool, saw notch to depth required. Raise sash and slide stool in position. Lower sash and draw line of sash on stool. Allow needed clearance between stool and window. Cut and nail stool in position with 6 penny finishing nails. Apron is optional, Illus. 26.

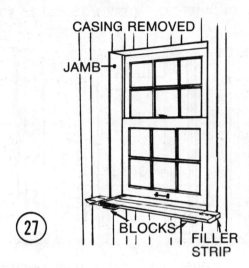

CASING REMOVED

JAMB

BLOCKS

FILLER STRIP

27

NOTE: When covering a jamb with paneling, Illus. 24, screw panel and stop in position. Do not use panel adhesive, glue or nails. This simplifies removing jamb and window if repairs are needed.

When applying new trim, Illus. 24, 25, use #2 molding at side and top. Miter cut side casing length required, apply glue and nail in position 3/16" from edge of jamb. Miter cut top casing. Apply glue, nail in position 3/16" from edge of jamb. When window is trimmed with casings, stool is cut to width of window, plus width of side casings, plus 2". This permits stool to project 1" beyond edge of casings.

When new casings are applied, use #2 molding for an apron.

Cut apron overall width of casings and nail in position. If gap between sash and existing jamb is greater than ¼", it will be necessary to screw a #8 stop, Illus. 25, after jamb has been covered with a strip of plywood.

In new construction, paneling on interior walls can be applied directly to studs. Always paint one inch of stud where panels butt together. Panels can be applied with adheisve or nails. A nailing machine, available on rental, speeds application. If plaster is to be applied on one side of a partition wall, prefinished paneling on the other, nail 2 x 4 cats between studs in position shown, Illus. 28. Cats help prevent studs from twisting. Apply #15 felt to studs before applying paneling.

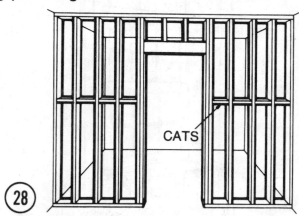

Insulate exterior walls with thickness insulation local conditions warrant, then staple #15 felt horizontally to studs. Overlap each course about 6". Use a stapling machine. This protects back of paneling from moisture. Use nails or veneer faced aluminum molding to apply paneling.

To avoid problems of dampness, always apply waterproofing to a concrete block or masonry wall before applying paneling. Your home improvement center can recommend a suitable product and directions for applying same.

Rather than nail furring strips directly to concrete block and puncture your wall, build a 2 x 4 frame to length and height required. Nail shoe and plate to studs with 16 penny nails, Illus. 29. Nail 1 x 2 blocks to back of frame. This spaces frame away from wall.

Place frame in position, check with level to make certain it's plumb, then wedge frame against ceiling joists by driving wood shingle or wedges cut to size required under shoe.

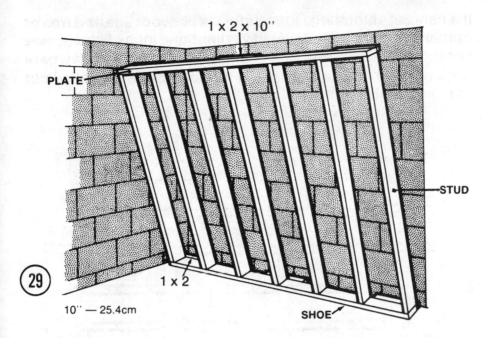

PLATE

1 x 2 x 10"

STUD

1 x 2

10" — 25.4cm

SHOE

Nail plate to ceiling joists. If ceiling joists run parallel to frame, nail 2 x 4 cats, 2 ft. on centers, Illus. 30, between joists. This installation will not disturb waterproofing seal on wall or floor.

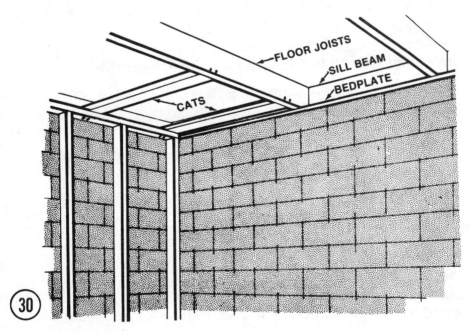

FLOOR JOISTS

SILL BEAM

BEDPLATE

CATS

31

If a concrete block wall foundation is above grade and free of dampness, cut 1 x 2 furring in 2 ft. lengths. Allow ½" breather space between ends. Allow for electrical conduit where required. Furring can be nailed to block walls with steel cut masonry nails, Illus. 31.

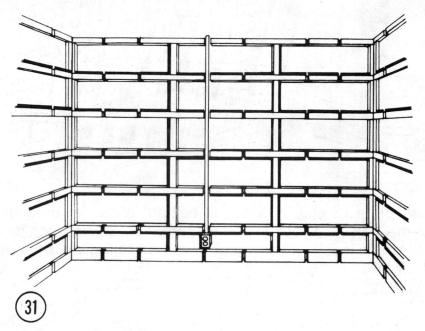

(31)

Never nail furring to concrete blocks below grade.

APPLYING PLYWOOD AROUND ARCHES

Use 1 x 2, 1 x 4, 1 x 6 or width furring required to frame arch, Illus. 32. Cut a strip of plywood width of A. This strip covers edge of furring. To bend A to curve required, make saw cuts ¾'' apart, through one ply, across bottomside, Illus. 33. Hold a scrap of 1 x 2 along each line, it simplifies making saw cut.

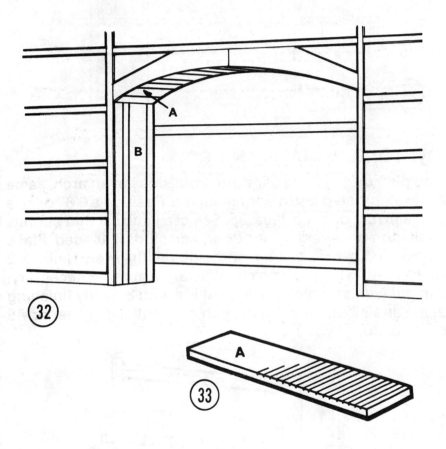

If two or more lengths of plywood are required to complete curve of arch, butt ends together. A sharper curve requires deeper cuts. Nail A to furring with 1'' brads or 4 penny finishing nails.

Cut matching lengths to cover B. 1 x 6 nailed across back of opening helps hold A in position. Wall panels cover edge of A and B, Illus. 34.

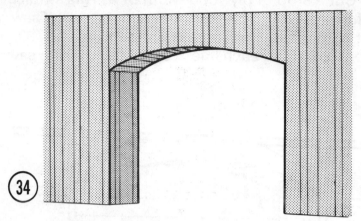

HOW TO ELIMINATE AN ARCH

If you plan on applying panels to both sides of an arch, same can be eliminated and a door installed. Position a 6'8" or size door jamb set desired, Illus. 35. Select a jamb set that permits installation of matching size door. Add studs if needed. Place in position, check header and sides with level. Nail 1 x 2 braces to hold square and even distance apart. If necessary, shim out with shingle. Nail in position with 8 penny finishing nails. Panels can be trimmed with cap, outside corner or #9 corner bead.

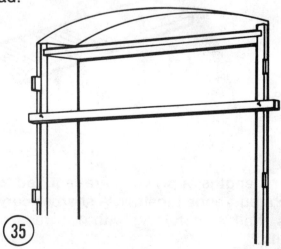

34

HOW TO PANEL WALLS OVER 8 FT.

4 x 10' panels are available in some wood grains. Where a ceiling is more than 8 ft., you can lower panel as much as 4" from ceiling, or raise panel as much as 8" from floor. Use matching panel for a wide ceiling trim or base, Illus. 36,37.

APPLICATION AT CEILING

CROWN MOLDING OR COVE   **BEVELED**   **QUARTER ROUND**

36

Place furring strips in position needed to support edge of panel. Use a strip of ¼" plywood to fur out to thickness required, Illus. 37.

APPLICATION AT FLOOR

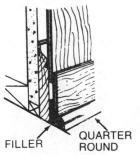

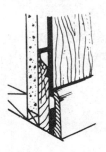

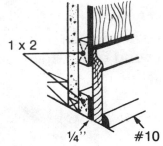

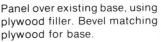

FILLER   QUARTER ROUND

1 x 2

¼"
6.4mm   #10

37

Panel over existing base, using plywood filler. Bevel matching plywood for base.

Panel over existing baseboard. Use #4 base.

Baseboard removed; furring nailed in place; old base replaced.

Another way to apply paneling in a high ceiling room is with a chair rail as explained on page 22.

ENCLOSING A POST

Posts in a basement can be enclosed as shown, Illus. 38. Nail 1 x 6 or width required, to 1 x 2 cut to length required, every 2 ft., full length of column. Cut panel to size required. Use #9 corner, #4 base or #5 shoe. Miter ends of base and shoe molding. Use matching trim at ceiling.

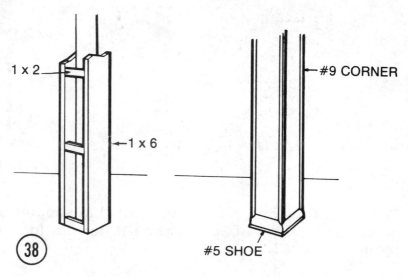

1 x 2

1 x 6

#9 CORNER

#5 SHOE

(38)

STAIRS

Paneling can butt against stair stringer, Illus. 39. #10 quarter round or #6 cove can be nailed in position shown.

#6 COVE

(39)

ENCLOSING PIPE, GIRDER, HEATING DUCT

A steel beam or girder can be enclosed in this manner. Nail 1 x 2 A alongside girder, Illus. 40. Cut ¼" plywood B to width and length required, Illus. 41. Nail B to 1 x 2 C spaced as shown. Cut ¼" plywood D to width and length required. Nail D to C. Raise assembled enclosure and nail D to A.

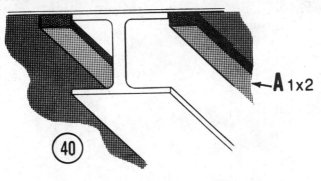

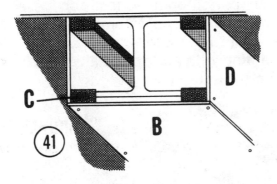

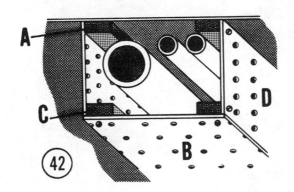

Follow same procedure when enclosing pipes and valves, Illus. 42, with the following changes. Pipes that contain shut off valves require inspection. Pipes also need air. Use pegboard for B and D. Screw D to A so entire enclosure can be removed.

Illus. 43 shows another way of enclosing pipe. Nail D to E and C. Screw B to C. Screw E to bottom of joist.

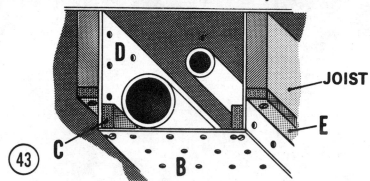

Heating and air conditioning ducts can be enclosed with framing shown, Illus. 44. Build frame to width required. Nail 1 x 2 A to joists. Cut 1 x 3 B to length required. Nail B to A, C to B. Cover framing with perforated aluminum or hardboard panels cut to size required.

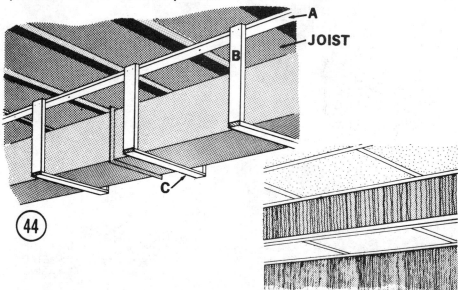

If joists run parallel to duct, nail B to joists.

TIPS OF THE TRADE

There are many ways prefinished plywood can be installed. An inside corner can be made by butting panels together, an outside corner by mitering panels, Illus. 45.

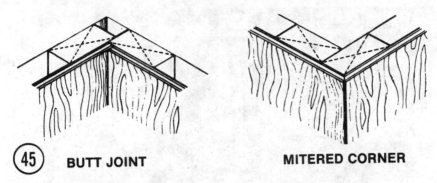

(45)   **BUTT JOINT**   **MITERED CORNER**

Illus. 46 shows panel over 1 x 2 furring. Existing trim around doors and windows remains exposed. Edge of panel is trimmed with ¼" quarter round.

Illus. 47 shows #2 casing applied on an outside corner.

Illus. 48 shows #1 cap molding combined with #2 casing.

Illus. 49 shows #2 casing rabbeted to receive ¼" panel.

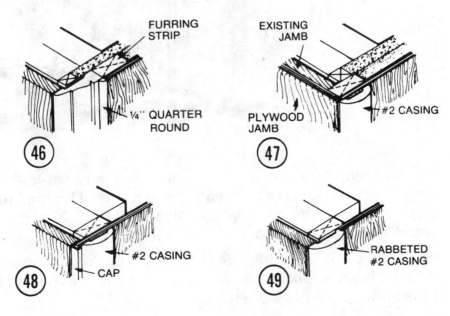

HOW TO BUILD WALL-TO-WALL CLOSETS

Transforming wall space into a sliding, hinged or bi-folding door storage closet isn't difficult. The small cost for material and hardware offers an economical solution to a really convenient storage area.

Prefinished paneling simplifies building doors. When matching panels are applied to adjacent walls, a decorator effect is achieved.

Since ample storage space is important to one's way of life, building hinged or sliding door storage, Illus. 51, 52, wall-to-wall, or from a window or door to a wall, Illus. 65, solves many needs.

52

A clothes storage closet should provide 22" minimum clear space I.D., inside dimensions. A sliding door closet framed as shown, Illus. 53, provides 26" I.D. This accommodates winter coats, etc. When hinged or bi-folding doors are to be installed, you can cut it down to 24" O.D., outside dimension.

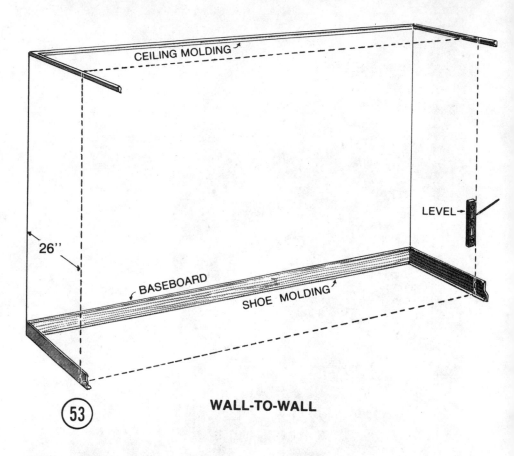

(53) **WALL-TO-WALL**

Measure 26" from wall and snap a chalk line on floor. Using a level, draw lines up walls, then snap a chalk line across ceiling. When facing frame is added, unit finishes 27" overall.

The baseboard on side and back wall and ceiling molding can be left intact. Build frame A, Illus. 54, to fit from top of baseboard to ceiling, or to ceiling molding. If you decide to remove baseboard and ceiling molding within area of unit, measure distance between floor and ceiling. Build frame A length required.

42

Build frame D to size required, Illus. 55. Use 1 x 4 and 1 x 2. Select lumber fairly free of knots. Cut 1 x 4 and 1 x 2 length required, apply glue and fasten with two ⅜" corrugated fasteners at each joint, Illus. 56. Check corners with square. Saw ¾ x 2½" notch for B, ¾ x 2½" for E, ¾" for F.

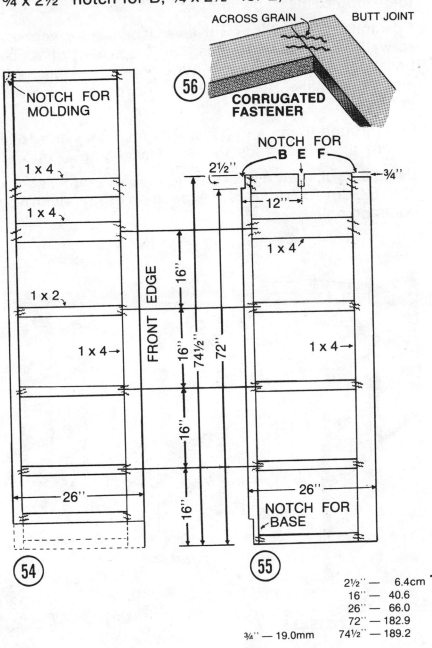

ACROSS GRAIN   BUTT JOINT

(56) CORRUGATED FASTENER

NOTCH FOR MOLDING

1 x 4

1 x 4

1 x 2

1 x 4

FRONT EDGE

26"

(54)

NOTCH FOR
B E F

2½"   ¾"

12"

1 x 4

1 x 4

26"

NOTCH FOR BASE

16"   16"   16"   16"   16"   74½"   72"

(55)

2½" —	6.4cm
16" —	40.6
26" —	66.0
72" —	182.9
¾" — 19.0mm 74½" —	189.2

43

When frame is square, use it as a pattern to cut ¼" plywood to size required.

Frame can either be spiked in position with 8 penny common nails, then covered with panel, or panel can be applied before toenailing frame in position.

Position frame A. Check with level. If necessary, scribe frame to wall (or baseboard), Illus. 58. Keep point of scriber on baseboard, pencil on frame. With coping or saber saw, saw along drawn line. Replace in position, check with level. Nail in place.

Nail through frame A into a corner stud. Measure 16" from corner to locate studs in wall. Nail frame D into stud.

Using a level, draw a level line to indicate bottom edge of B, Illus. 57. Cut 1 x 3 for B. Nail in position to studs with 8 penny common nails.

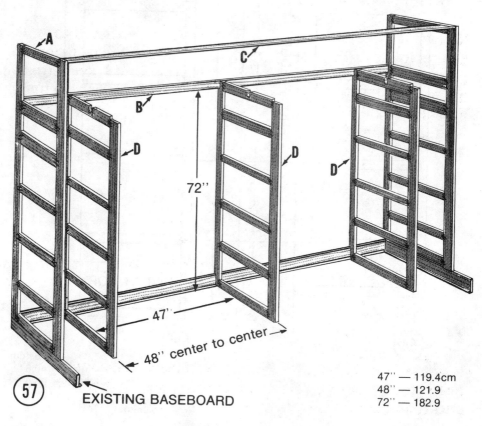

57 EXISTING BASEBOARD

72"

47'

48" center to center

47" — 119.4cm
48" — 121.9
72" — 182.9

44

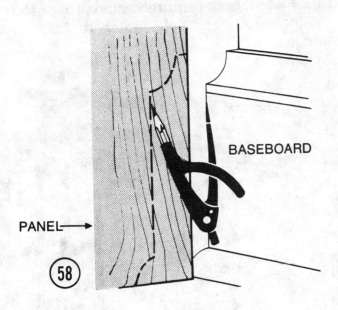

BASEBOARD

PANEL→

(58)

Nail 1 x 4 C to ceiling in position indicated. Toenail to A. If ceiling joists run crosswise to C, nail C to joists with 16 penny common nails. Since joists are usually spaced 16" on center, measure 16" from wall, test with a 4 or 6 penny finishing nail. If joists run parallel to C, fasten C to ceiling with toggle bolts, Illus. 59.

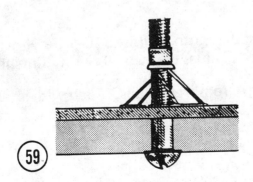

(59)

If necessary, notch D, Illus. 55, to receive baseboard. Saw notch for B, E and F to size of lumber used. Check with level and toenail D in place with 6 penny finishing nails.

45

Cut 1 x 3 E and 1 x 4 F to length required and nail in position, Illus. 60. Cut ¼" plywood for shelf. Notch to fit. Nail in position. Countersink nails.

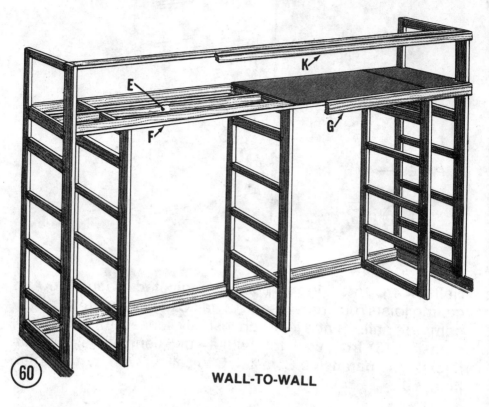

WALL-TO-WALL

Cut 1 x 2 H, Illus. 62, length required. Center H over D. Cut and nail 1 x 2 K to C, Illus. 60, with 6 penny finishing nails.

Cut 1 x 4 G to length required. Nail G flush with shelf. Screw ¼" sliding door track, Illus. 61, to top of G and to bottom of K. (Use size to fit plywood.)

Cut and toenail 1 x 2 L, Illus. 62.

Cut matching plywood to size required to veneer exposed edge and face of G,H,L,K.

Scribe panel to baseboard, Illus. 58, and with a coping or saber saw, cut to shape required.

46

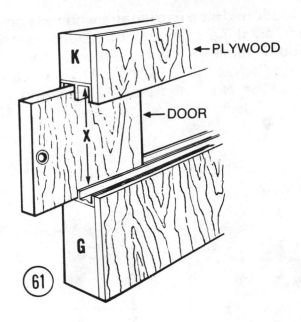

PLYWOOD

K

DOOR

X

G

(61)

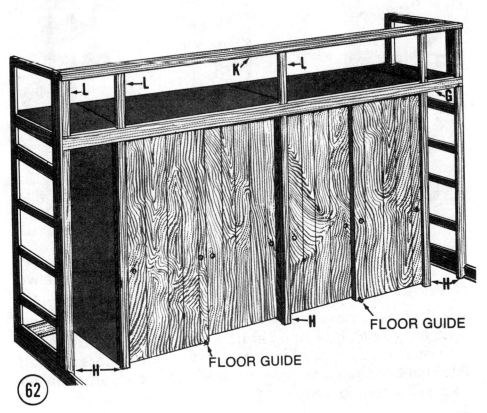

L

L

K

L

G

H

FLOOR GUIDE

H

FLOOR GUIDE

H

(62)

47

Illus. 63 shows framing required when space at ends doesn't warrant installing a hinged door. Build frames as previously outlined. Toenail 1 x 4 M in position to floor and F. If space N is 11¼" or less, a 1 x 12 can be cut to size required and nailed to M, Illus. 64. No other framing is required. Face frame with paneling, Illus.65.

(63)

When unit is built with an exposed end, Illus. 65, nail ¼" paneling to end before applying to front. A decorative molding can be used to trim cabinet at ceiling.

Buy or make doors to size of opening X, Illus. 63, less 1¾". This allows ¼" clearance at floor, 1½" clearance at top. If necessary, clearance at top can be 1¼". Build doors one half width of opening, plus ½". When two 2'0" doors are installed in a 47" opening, they overlap 1".

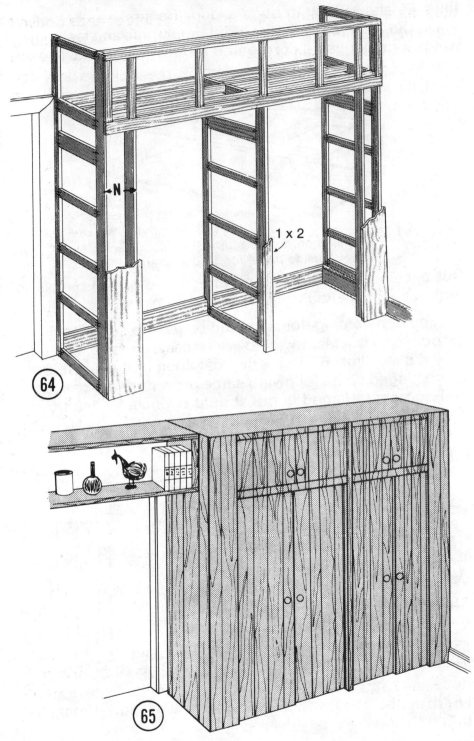

64

65

49

Illus. 66 shows how to build a door frame using 5/4 x 4 or 1 x 4. Cut A and B to size required. Apply glue and fasten butt joints together using corrugated fasteners, Illus. 56, in each corner.

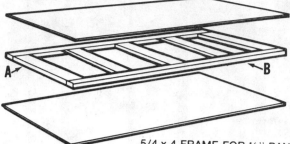

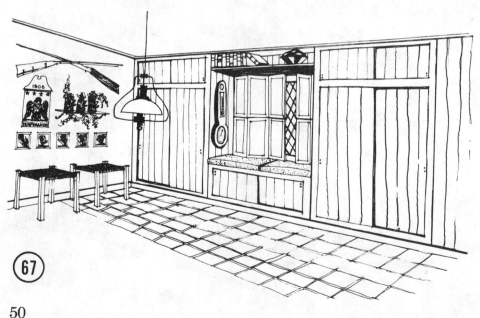

(66) 5/4 x 4 FRAME FOR ⅛" PANELS = 1⅜" DOOR
¾ x 4 FRAME FOR ¼" PANELS = 1¼" DOOR
½" flakeboard core plus ¼" plywood facing for ¾" door, add ¼" inside panel for 1" door hardware, Illus. 68.

Cut paneling to size frame requires. Glue or nail panels to both faces. Panel adhesive requires no nails.

Hinged or bi-folding doors should be built to size that clears carpeting by ¼". Many wall-to-wall closets are built on a 1 x 4 raised base, Illus. 67. Carpeting can then butt against base. Build hinged doors following same procedure described for sliding doors. Hinged doors should be installed with three cabinet door hinges.

(67)

Illus. 68, 69 shows sliding door track. Fasten track in position noted.

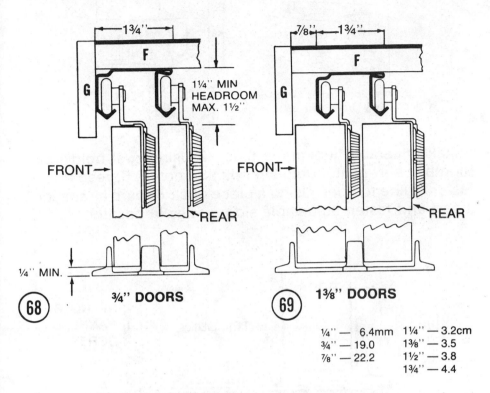

¼" — 6.4mm	1¼" — 3.2cm
¾" — 19.0	1⅜" — 3.5
⅞" — 22.2	1½" — 3.8
	1¾" — 4.4

Fasten door hangers 2" from edge, Illus. 70, or distance manufacturer of hardware specifies. Illus. 90c shows another type of sliding door hardware.

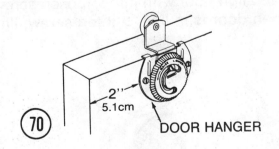

Hang rear door first by tilting top of door, Illus. 71, then install front door.

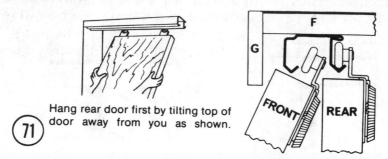

Hang rear door first by tilting top of door away from you as shown.

Install adjustable floor guide, Illus. 72. Using level, hold doors plumb, insert center guide in position noted. Spread doors, fasten guide to floor. Using a piece of cardboard as spacer,* insert and fasten adjustable side guides in position.

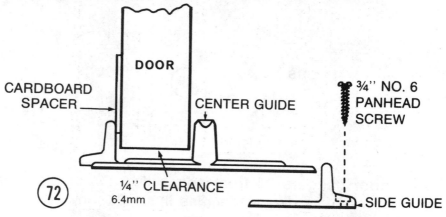

If necessary to align door with jamb, loosen screw, Illus. 70, turn dial. When door is in line, tighten screw, Illus. 73.

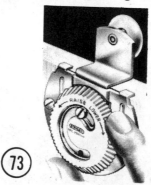

*Approx. 1/16" thick.

TOP CABINETS

Sliding doors can be installed in cabinets above clothes area, Illus. 61, 74, or same can be hinged. ¼" panels can be cut to size required. Aluminum or plastic track is cut to length required. The wide section of track is installed at top. Use screws supplied.

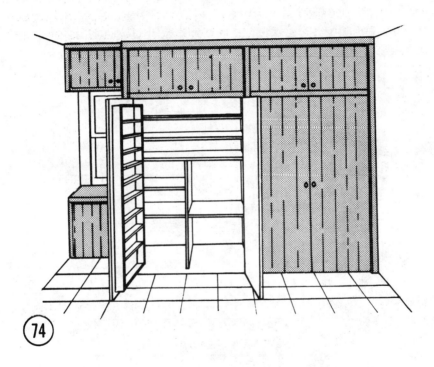

Cut panels ½ width of opening plus ½". This permits panels to overlap. Cut panels height of X, Illus. 61. Drill ¾" holes and install door pulls 1" from edge, center from top to bottom.

FLOOR TO CEILING DOORS

(75)

A currently popular design specifies doors built to fit between floor and ceiling, Illus. 75. Assemble frames using 1 x 4, Illus. 66. Cover both faces with prefinished plywood. These are installed with pivot hinges, Illus. 76. A pivot hinge is limited only by the overall weight of the door. Check weight limitation of the pivot hinges you purchase, then watch your weight. Pivot hinges are available for 1¼, 1⅜" or thicker door, weighing up to 100 lbs.

54

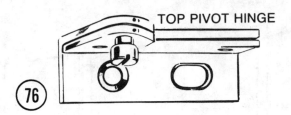

TOP PIVOT HINGE

76

Pivot hinges can be installed in three different ways. Illus. 77 shows flush mounted; Illus. 78, recessed; Illus. 79, overlay. We recommend flush mounted.

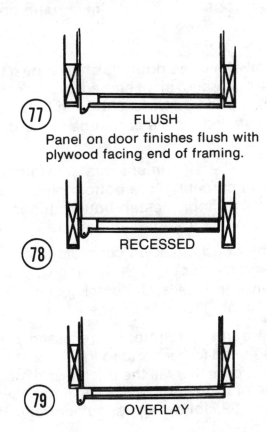

77 FLUSH

Panel on door finishes flush with plywood facing end of framing.

78 RECESSED

79 OVERLAY

Hinges are available for left or right hand mounting. A right hand door opens from right, Illus. 80; hinges are mounted on left as you face the door. Hinges for this opening are marked RHT — Right Hand Top; RHB — Right Hand Bottom.

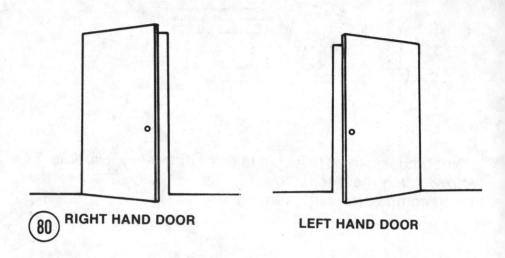

(80) RIGHT HAND DOOR   **LEFT HAND DOOR**

Framing for a pivot hinged door closet is shown in Illus. 81. Divide space by number of pivot hinged doors desired. Doors up to 1⅜" thick, up to 3 ft. wide, and from floor to ceiling in height can be installed. Space partitions P to width required to accommodate doors.

Build frames to overall dimensions previously outlined. When there is no carpeting, the bottom pivot hinge can be fastened directly to floor. Fasten bottom hinge to a ¾" or thicker plywood block if floor is carpeted.

Use a thicker plywood block on concrete floors. This must take the ¾" screws supplied with hinges. Nail block to concrete with masonry nails. Cut block just large enough to accommodate hinge, Illus. 76.

You can install a flush mounted or recessed pivot hinged door to a block nailed to floor and to the 5/4 x 1½" rail, Illus. 81, across top. Recess this rail the thickness of door plus ¼" from front edge of frame. Allow ⅛" spacing between hinge and frame, Illus. 82, following manufacturer's directions.

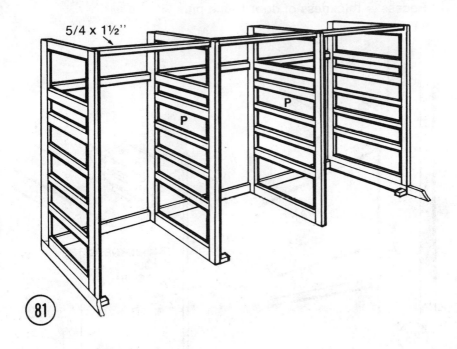

5/4 x 1½''

P

P

(81)

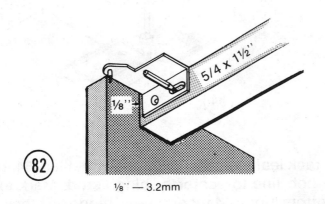

5/4 x 1½''

⅛''

(82)

⅛'' — 3.2mm

57

Take hinge apart. Place in position indicated. Locate and mark center of elongated hole. Remove hinge and draw lines shown, Illus. 83.

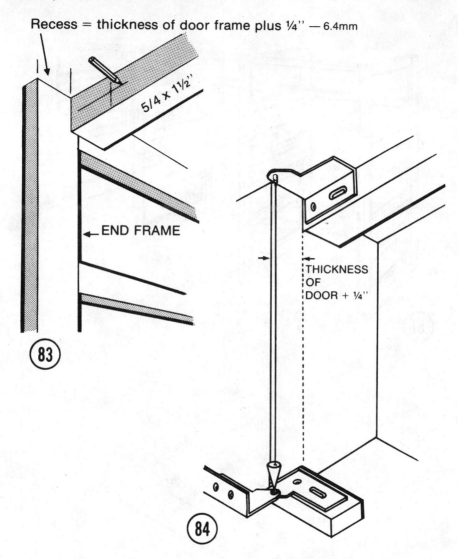

Recess = thickness of door frame plus ¼" — 6.4mm

5/4 x 1½"

←END FRAME

THICKNESS
OF
DOOR + ¼"

83

84

Replace and tack leaf temporarily in position, Illus. 84. Hold or tie plumb bob line to center of hinge stud. Mark exact position of bottom hinge. Mark outline of hinge on block and outline of block on floor. Fasten block to floor. Drill a pilot hole for screw in elongated hole.

The top and bottom hinge leaf can be mounted on edge or mortised into door. If you mortise, use a hinge leaf as a pattern, Illus. 85. Chisel mortise thickness of leaf. Keep leaf flush with inside face of door. NOTE: Always follow pivot hinge manufacturer's directions.

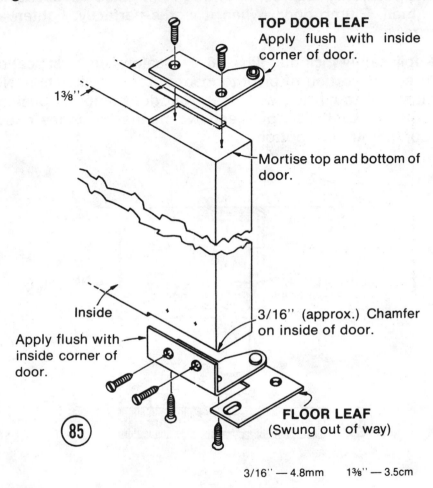

TOP DOOR LEAF
Apply flush with inside corner of door.

1⅜"

Mortise top and bottom of door.

Inside

Apply flush with inside corner of door.

3/16" (approx.) Chamfer on inside of door.

(85)

FLOOR LEAF
(Swung out of way)

3/16" — 4.8mm   1⅜" — 3.5cm

Chamfer inside bottom edge of door about 3/16" to accommodate shape of hinge, Illus. 85.

The overall height of door depends on whether you mortise hinge leaf at top and bottom. A flush mounting requires amount of space hinge manufacturer specifies. This can be ⅜" at top, ⅜" at bottom. The door would be ¾" less in overall height than opening Y, Illus. 86.

59

With top leaf positioned ⅛" from end frame, attach with screw in position indicated, Illus. 84, to 5/4 x 1½" stop. Do not tighten screw all the way. Fasten top and bottom leaf to door. With door open, insert top leaf on stud, slide bottom into position. Fasten screw through elongated slot but do not tighten. Plumb door. When it works perfectly, tighten all screws.

Apply safety lock nut, Illus. 86. The safety nut must seat on threaded portion of pivot to insure proper installation. Nut must not touch top door leaf. Nail door stops in position required. Apply door pulls and two magnetic catches, one at top, the other at bottom.

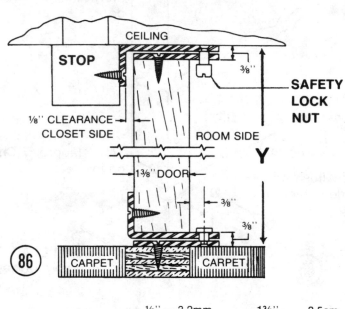

⅛" — 3.2mm	1⅜" — 3.5cm
⅜" — 9.5	16" — 40.6
	32½" — 82.6
	6'10" — 208.3

FREE-STANDING CABINET WITH BASE

A clothes cabinet on casters or glides can be built in the following manner. Build two frames D, Illus. 87. Do not notch for base. Families that need to create an extra bedroom, build these to room height less 1". When placed end to end, they make a convenient room divider.

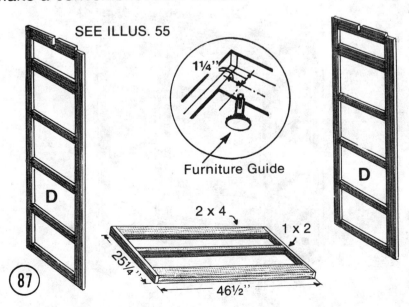

SEE ILLUS. 55

1¼"

Furniture Guide

D

D

2 x 4

1 x 2

25¼"

46½"

87

Build base and back frames to size indicated, Illus. 88.

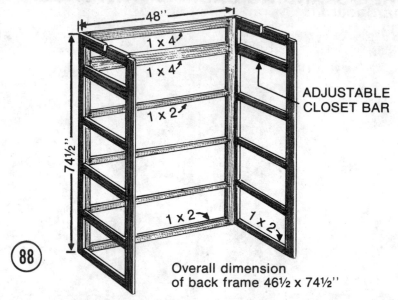

ADJUSTABLE
CLOSET BAR

48"

74½"

1 x 4
1 x 4
1 x 2
1 x 2
1 x 2

Overall dimension
of back frame 46½ x 74½"

(88)

Space 1 x 2 and 1 x 4 as shown, Illus. 88, 89. Casters, Illus. 90a, can be bolted to 2 x 4 base in position shown.

Apply glue and nail side frames to back and base with 8 penny finishing nails. Nail 1 x 3 N, 1 x 4 P and R in position shown, Illus. 89, 90, 90c. Cut 1 x 6 to width required for R if sliding door hardware requires a wide fascia.

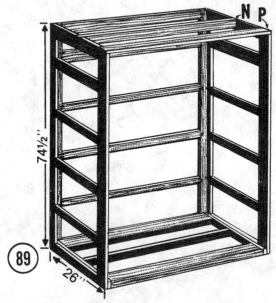

N P

74½"

26"

(89)

Cut and nail 1 x 3 S and 1 x 2 T in position, Illus. 90. Cut ⅛''
hardboard to overall size of back. Glue and nail in position.
Cut 3/16 or ¼'' hardboard for floor. Nail in position. Cut ¼''
prefinished plywood to size required for back, sides and to
face R, S and T.

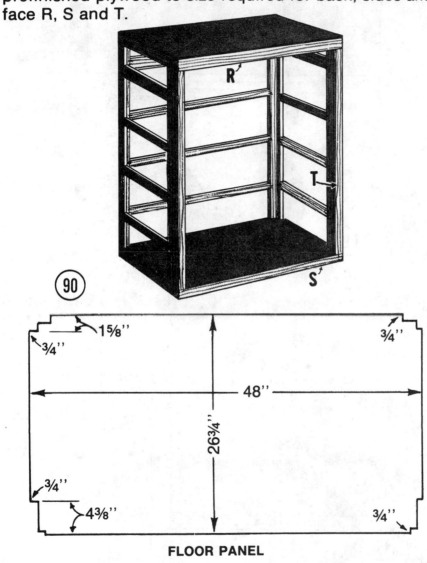

FLOOR PANEL

Build and install doors following procedure previously
outlined. Line inside of cabinet with ⅛'' standard hardboard
or pegboard following procedure previously outlined. Install
closet bar, Illus. 90b.

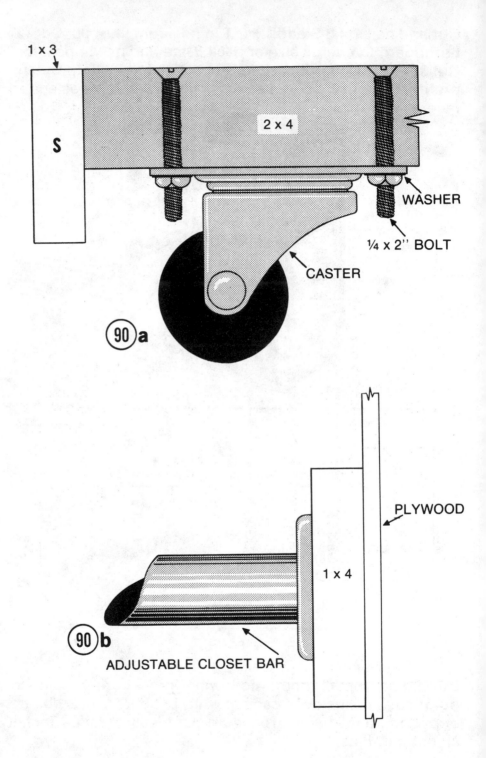

1 x 3

S

2 x 4

WASHER

¼ x 2'' BOLT

CASTER

90 a

PLYWOOD

1 x 4

90 b

ADJUSTABLE CLOSET BAR

64

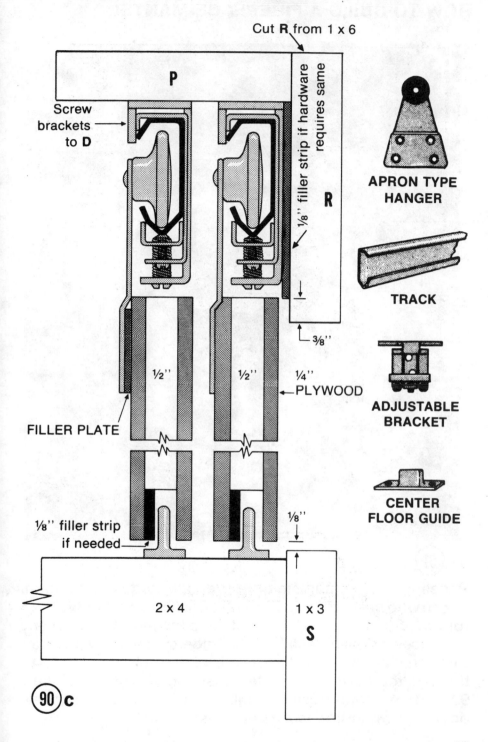

Cut **R** from 1 x 6

P

Screw brackets to **D**

¹⁄₈'' filler strip if hardware requires same

R

³⁄₈''

½'' ½''

¼''
←PLYWOOD

FILLER PLATE

¹⁄₈''

¹⁄₈'' filler strip if needed

2 x 4

1 x 3

S

APRON TYPE HANGER

TRACK

ADJUSTABLE BRACKET

CENTER FLOOR GUIDE

(90) c

65

HOW TO BUILD A FIREPLACE MANTEL

(91)

Paneling a room containing a fireplace adds great charm. Those who need a fireplace mantel will find directions easy to follow. Stain mantel to match paneling. Since many fireplaces contain metal air chambers that draw cold air through openings at floor level, and discharge warm air through top ports, the mantel must contain openings, Illus. 92, to size and in position required. Hinged doors conceal openings when fireplace isn't in use, Illus. 91.

As fireplaces vary in width and height, the materials listed are ample for the 36" wide by 27" opening.

1 — ¼ x 30 x 72" plywood for #1, #2
1 — 1 x 8 x 12' for #3, #5, #6
1 — 1 x 3 x 6' for #4
1 — 5/4 x 8 x 4' for #7, #8
8 ft. ¾ x 2½" door trim molding #9
8 ft. 1¾" x 2" crown molding #11
3 ft. ¾" nosing #12
½ lb. 8 penny finishing nails
¼ lb. 4 penny finishing nails
1 box 1¼" No. 17 brads
Glue
4 prs. 1 x 1½" tight pin butt hinges for doors
14' #10 molding
3' #13 molding
3' #14 molding

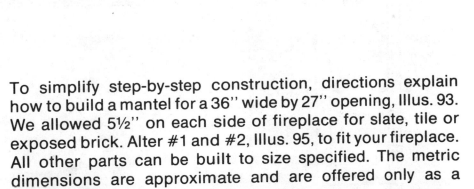

To simplify step-by-step construction, directions explain how to build a mantel for a 36" wide by 27" opening, Illus. 93. We allowed 5½" on each side of fireplace for slate, tile or exposed brick. Alter #1 and #2, Illus. 95, to fit your fireplace. All other parts can be built to size specified. The metric dimensions are approximate and are offered only as a general guide.

The overall height of the mantel shown, Illus. 93, is 52¾" by 68¼" wide.

Illus. 94 shows location of each numbered part and material used. It also shows full size end view of moldings used on sample mantel. All material is available in lumber yards. If ¾" matching hardwood plywood is available, it can be used for #1 and #2. Or you can use ¾" fir plywood and stain it to match paneling on wall. Or ½" fir plywood can be covered with ¼" paneling.

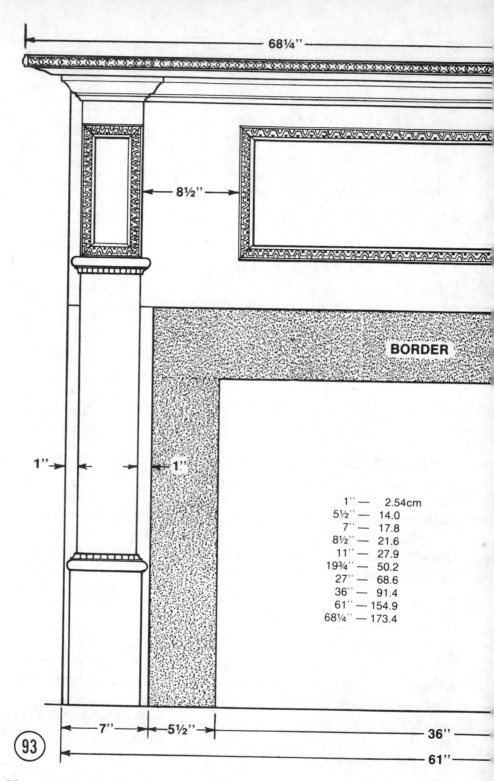

68¼"

8½"

BORDER

1"

1"

1"	—	2.54cm
5½"	—	14.0
7"	—	17.8
8½"	—	21.6
11"	—	27.9
19¾"	—	50.2
27"	—	68.6
36"	—	91.4
61"	—	154.9
68¼"	—	173.4

7"

5½"

36"

61"

93

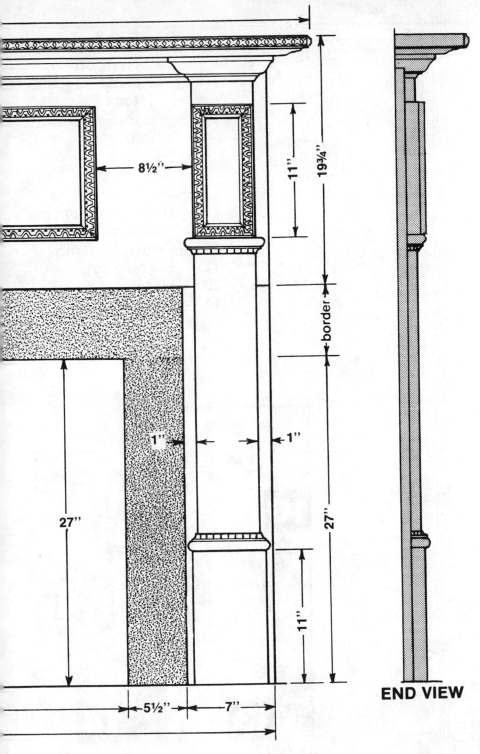

8½"

11"

19¾"

border

1"   1"

27"

27"

11"

5½"   7"

END VIEW

69

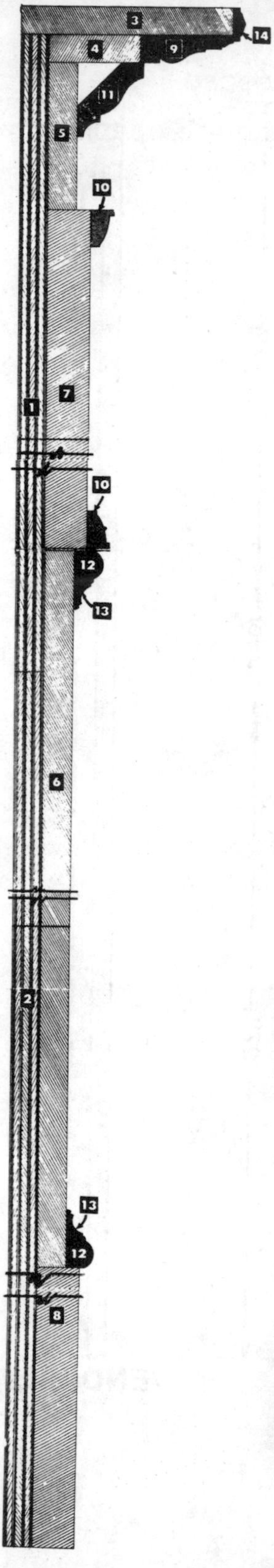

PARTS LIST

1 — ¾'' plywood
2 — ¾'' plywood
3 — 1'' stock
4 — 1'' stock
5 — 1'' stock
6 — 1'' stock
7 — 5/4'' stock
8 — 5/4'' stock
9 — Door trim molding
10 — Molding
11 — Crown molding
12 — ¾'' nosing
13 — Molding
14 — Molding

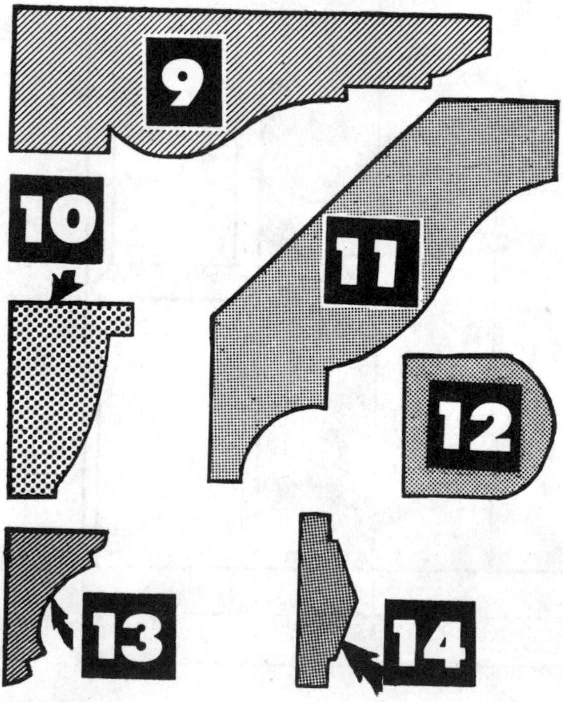

94

Cut #1, Illus. 95, 19" wide to length needed.

Cut #2, 7" wide by length equal to fireplace opening, plus width of top border, Illus. 95. All other parts are cut to size noted regardless of any change in size of #1 and #2.

Cut #1, Illus. 95, for a 36 x 27" opening, 19 x 61". The length of #1 is estimated by adding width of fireplace opening (36") plus two borders 11", plus 14".

Cut two #2, Illus. 95, 7 x 33" or length required. #2 is equal to height of opening, plus height of top border. If fireplace contains cold air intakes, cut opening in #2 to size and position required.

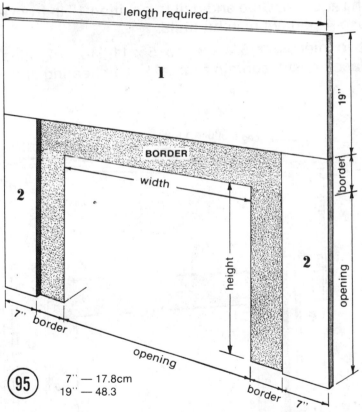

length required

1

19"

BORDER

border

width

2

height

2

opening

7" border

opening

border 7"

95 7" — 17.8cm
    19" — 48.3

Apply glue and fasten #1 and #2 in position using ½ x 1½" corrugated fasteners driven in back face. Allow glue to set. Place assembled #1 and #2 in position. Check with level and nail in place with 8 penny finishing nails driven into studs.

71

Cut #3 from 1 x 8 to 5⅝" width, Illus. 96, to length of #1, plus 6". This allows 3" projection on each side. Apply glue and nail in position to top edge of #1 with 8 penny finishing nails.

Cut #4, Illus. 96, from 1 x 3 — 2⅜" wide by 1" longer than #1. Apply glue and toenail #4 to #1 allowing #4 to project ½" beyond #1 at both ends.

Cut two #5, Illus. 96, from 1 x 8 — 5" wide by 4" long. Apply glue and nail in position with 4 penny finishing nails. #5 is recessed 1" from edge of #1.

Locate and mark position of #6, Illus. 96. Locate #6 — 11" below #5 and 11" up from bottom. Cut two pieces 5" wide by length required. Glue and nail in position 1" in from edge of #2. Use 4 penny finishing nails.

Cut two pieces of 5/4 x 8" to 5 x 11" for #7, Illus. 97. If fireplace doesn't contain a metal hot air heating unit, nail #7

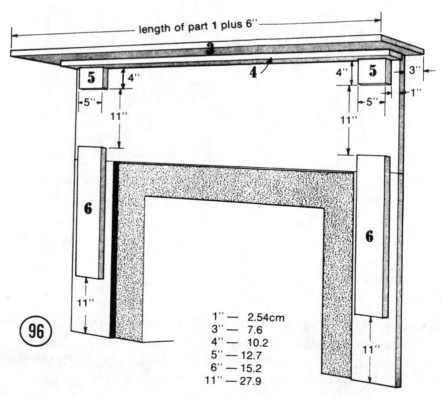

length of part 1 plus 6"

1" — 2.54cm
3" — 7.6
4" — 10.2
5" — 12.7
6" — 15.2
11" — 27.9

in position shown with 4 penny finishing nails. If fireplace contains a hot air chamber, #7 and #8 become doors and are hinged in position with 1 x 1½" tight pin hinges.

Cut two pieces of 5/4 x 8" to 6 x 11" for #8, Illus. 97. Glue and nail in position ½" in from edge of #2 using 4 penny finishing nails, or hinge in position as noted above.

Miter cut molding #9, Illus. 94, 97, same length as #3. Apply glue and nail in position with 1¼" brads. Position #9 flush with front edge of #3. Miter cut one end of two additional 5⅝" lengths of same molding. Apply glue and nail in position at ends, Illus. 97.

Miter cut four pieces of molding #10, Illus. 97, to 11", 4 pieces 5". Apply glue and nail in position with 1¼" brads. Miter cut two additional 11" lengths. Nail in position for center panel. Miter cut two pieces to length required and nail in place.

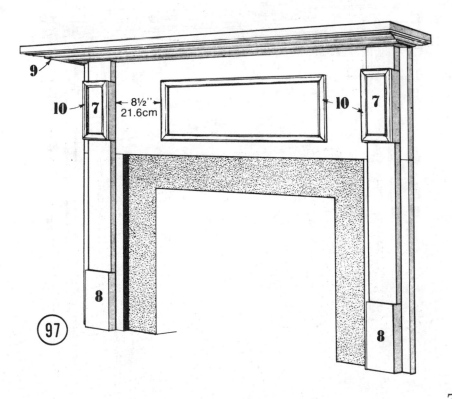

Miter cut, glue and nail crown molding #11, Illus. 94, 98, 99, with 1¼" brads. Fasten long length in place, then cut shorter pieces to fit. Molding #11 butts against wall. It is notched to fit around #1, Illus. 99.

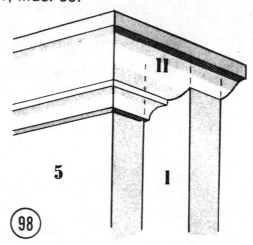

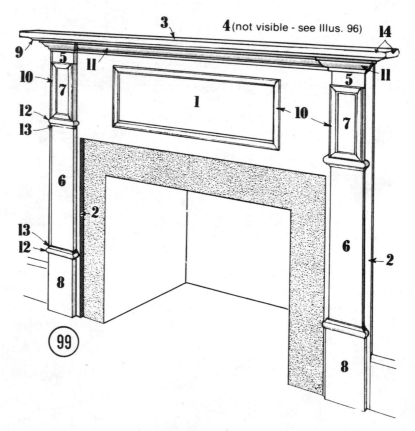

4 (not visible - see Illus. 96)

Miter cut, glue and nail ¾" nosing #12, Illus. 94, 99, in position indicated with 1¼" brads. Follow same procedure and apply ½" cove molding #13, Illus. 94, 99.

Miter cut ends of molding #14, Illus. 94, 99. Nail to front edge and ends of #3 with 1¼" brads. Ends butt against wall.

If baseboard in room has a molding on top, this can be continued up side of #2 and #1.

Set all nails. Fill holes. Touch up with matching Putty Stik.

If 5/4" lumber is difficult to obtain, use 1" lumber and cover with ¼" prefinished plywood.

If metal grilles can't easily be removed from openings, mortise out back of #1 and #2 about 3/16" to receive grille. Don't permit wood to come in direct contact with metal. Cover edge of grille with a strip of asbestos.

When hinging doors, mortise edge of #7 and #8 to receive full thickness of hinge. Doors can be held in closed position with a bullet type door catch.

EASY TO BUILD DECORATIVE VALANCES

(100)

Prefinished paneling simplifies making valance and cornice boards. Install a valance, Illus. 100, when space between casing, Illus. 101, and ceiling is 12" or more. Install a cornice against ceiling, Illus. 102, when space is less than 12".

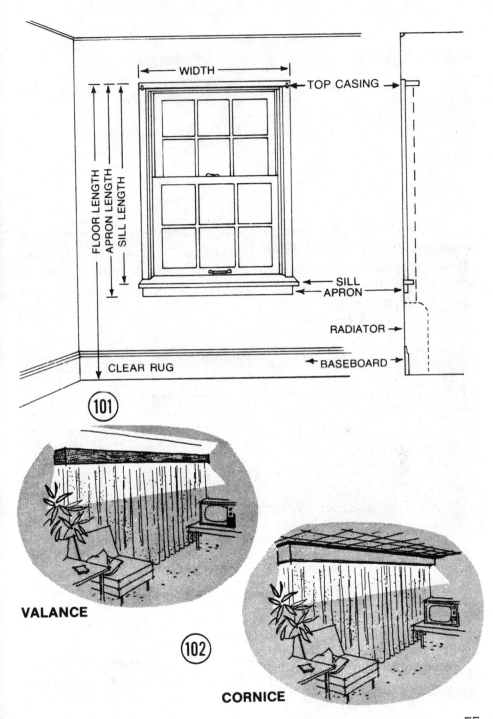

WIDTH

TOP CASING

FLOOR LENGTH

APRON LENGTH

SILL LENGTH

SILL

APRON

RADIATOR →

CLEAR RUG

← BASEBOARD

(101)

VALANCE

(102)

CORNICE

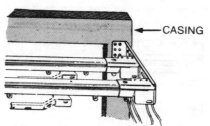

CASING

(103) **LONG PROJECTION OR DOUBLE TRAVERSE ROD KIT**

Traverse track, also called traverse rod, may be fastened directly to the casing, Illus. 103, or to 1 x 3 or 1 x 4 F, Illus. 104, nailed across top of casing. Those who want to dramatize draperies or complement a narrow window can add 6 to 10" to each side.

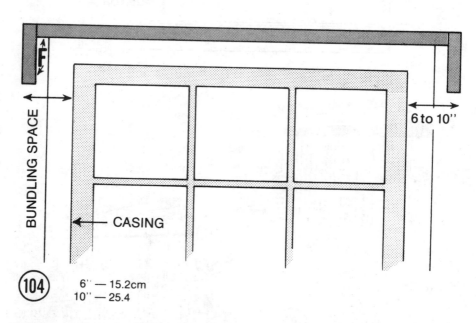

BUNDLING SPACE

6 to 10"

CASING

(104)   6" — 15.2cm
         10" — 25.4

Hang a drapery panel, as it would normally be hung, at side of window. Measure space it requires. Cut top F to length drapery panel requires.

78

Illus. 101 shows the various dimensions you will need when you shop for draperies, curtains, traverse track and indirect lighting channel.

Illus. 105 shows an easy to build cornice that contains ample space for a traverse rod as well as fluorescent channel.

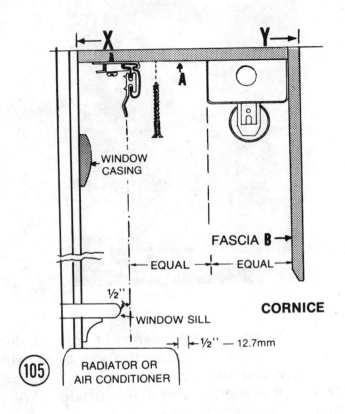

Valance and cornice boards that are to be painted or covered with fabric can be made from 1 x 6, 1 x 8, 1 x 10, etc. If you plan on covering with ¼'' prefinished plywood, cut all parts from ½'' plywood.

An ornate, decorator style valance, Illus. 106, can be made from carved wood molding and prefinished plywood. Directions for building these are offered on page 95.

(106)

Before starting to measure for a valance or cornice, decide what hardware, i.e., single or double traverse track, with or without fluorescent channel, you want to install. Illus. 107 shows hardware for draperies and glass curtains. Illus. 108 shows position of lighting channel.

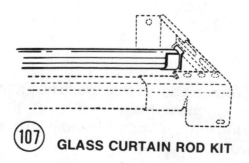

(107) **GLASS CURTAIN ROD KIT**

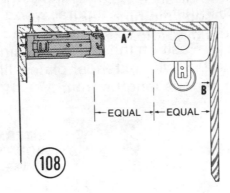

A'

B

|← EQUAL →|← EQUAL →|

(108)

If you plan on extending draperies, you will want a window widener kit, Illus. 109. The ceiling of a valance or cornice board is cut to width required, Illus. 105, 108. Always position traverse track so it permits drapery or curtain to clear a window sill, radiator or air conditioner by a minimum of ½'', Illus. 105. As the cost of fuel goes up, draperies that completely enclose a window save fuel. Those that blank off a radiator enhance the decor while they increase fuel costs. Traverse track should be positioned a channel width away from a fluorescent fixture.

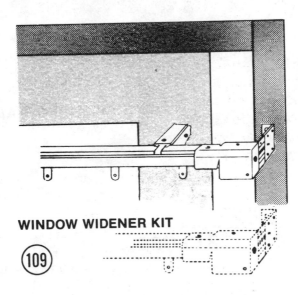

WINDOW WIDENER KIT

(109)

81

Illus. 110 shows various parts supplied with most traverse track sets. Those installing a natural wood or prefinished plywood valance, or a fabric valance, should install valance rod kits, Illus. 111. Position these above casing, Illus. 112, or to the side, Illus. 113, with extender plates, Illus. 114. These are available in various lengths from 6, 9, 12 to 18''.

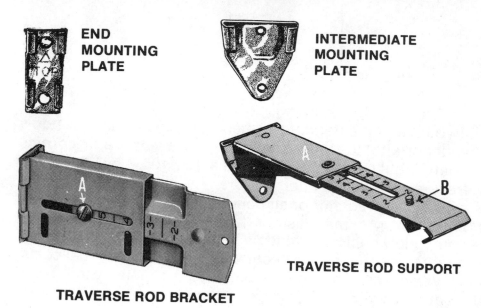

END MOUNTING PLATE

INTERMEDIATE MOUNTING PLATE

TRAVERSE ROD SUPPORT

TRAVERSE ROD BRACKET

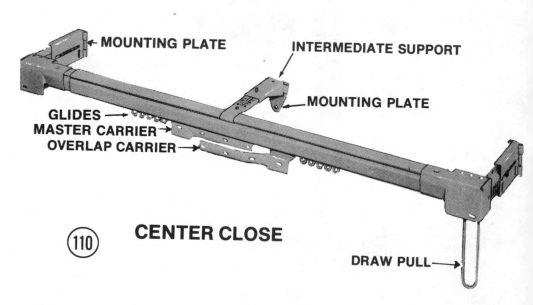

MOUNTING PLATE

INTERMEDIATE SUPPORT

MOUNTING PLATE

GLIDES
MASTER CARRIER
OVERLAP CARRIER

CENTER CLOSE

(110)

DRAW PULL

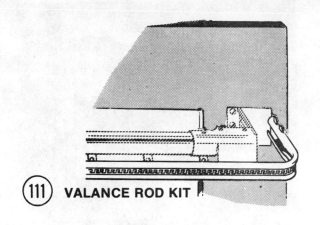

(111) VALANCE ROD KIT

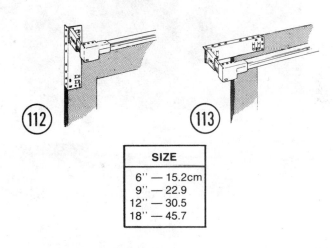

(112)   (113)

SIZE
6" — 15.2cm
9" — 22.9
12" — 30.5
18" — 45.7

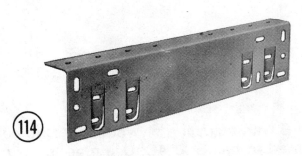

(114)

EXTENDER PLATE

83

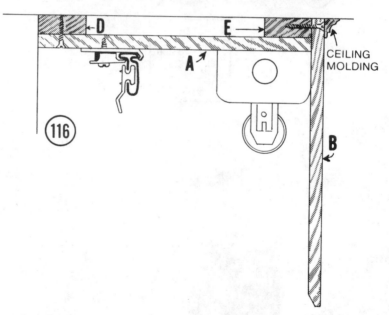

CEILING
MOLDING

If you cover B with matching plywood, cut B to height and length required to nail B to AC. Use glue to face BC with prefinished plywood.

Full size patterns on foldout sheet simplify building decorative valance boards, Illus. 115, 117, 128. Use carbon paper to trace pattern onto a large sheet of paper. Cut the paper pattern to shape shown. Place it against the window. Extend width or depth to suit your needs. When the pattern is acceptable, trace along edge on lumber specified.

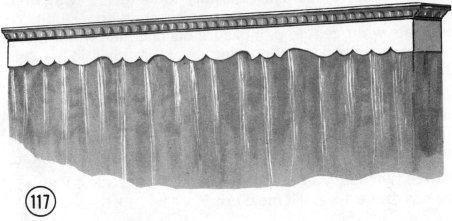

(117)

Step by step directions, plus these full size templates greatly simplify building.

While fascia board B, Illus. 105, can be 6, 8 or 10" in width, many decorators recommend up to 12". Always note width of a valance board that is pleasing. Note its height from floor and/or ceiling. Make yours same width. Extra height can be added to fascia B by nailing A to B, Illus. 118.

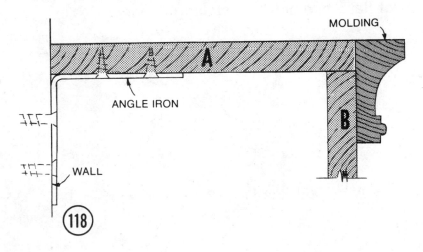

MOLDING

A

ANGLE IRON

B

WALL

(118)

2 to 4'' angle brackets, Illus. 118, greatly simplify installing valance boards to casing around window. When used to fasten cornice boards, use long enough screws to drive into studs.

As indicated in Illus. 105, 108, the traverse track must be positioned so glides allow drapery to hang ½'' away from edge of a window sill, radiator or air conditioner unit. To estimate width required, measure distance the window sill, radiator or air conditioner projects from casing. Add ½''. This distance should be plumb with glides on traverse track.

Prior to making a valance or cornice, draw this distance on ceiling of valance or cornice. Those wishing to install fluorescent channel should draw another line double the width of channel away from glide. Cut A to width required.

NOTE: When lumber is specified, i.e., 1 x 2, 1 x 6, 1 x 8, etc., we assume a 1 x 2 will measure ¾ x 1½'', 1 x 6 — ¾ x 5½'', 1 x 8 — ¾ x 7¼''.

Valance boards can be made from 1'' lumber, ½, ⅝ or ¾'' plywood for A, C; ⅛'' hardboard, ¼'' plywood or 1'' lumber for B. Always cut B to length required. Cut A length of B, less 1½'', Illus. 119, when 1'' lumber is used. Cut C to width of A and to height of B. Apply glue and nail B to C and A using 4 penny finishing nails. Nail C to A. Those who wish to install fluorescent channels should paint inside surface with two coats of flat white before installing channel.

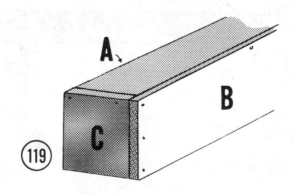

86

If length of valance requires joining two pieces end to end, apply glue, butt ends, fasten in position with a gusset plate. Glue and screw gusset plate in position shown, Illus. 120. Cut gusset to width required to allow space for channel.

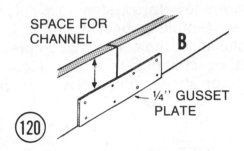

If you need to join fluorescent channel end to end, Illus. 121, follow channel manufacturer's directions.

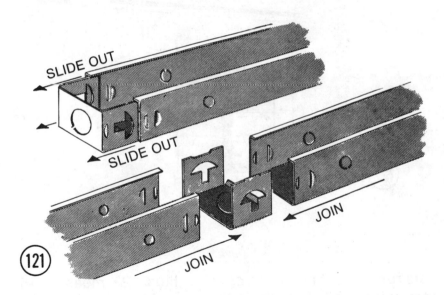

Since a valance containing traverse rod for draperies and channel for fluorescent fixture must support considerable weight, plus the pull when drawing draperies, fasten a valance to a 1 x 3 or 1 x 4 F, Illus. 104, fastened securely to studs in wall or to casing. This permits nailing valance through A and C into F.

A cornice should be fastened through ceiling into joists. Where joists run parallel to cornice, Illus. 122, fasten 1 x 3 or 1 x 4 D and E to ceiling with expansion bolts. These usually require drilling ⅜", or size hole specified, through D and E and ceiling. When installing fluorescent channels, make installation in cornice before fastening to ceiling. Book #694 Electrical Repairs Simplified provides much helpful information. In this installation, the ceiling A, complete with traverse track and lighting channel, is screwed to D and E. B is screwed in position shown, finished with molding, Illus. 116.

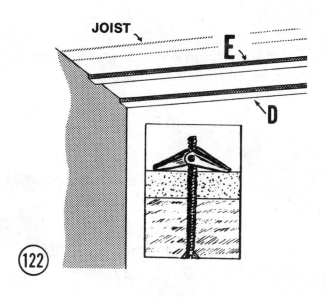

JOIST

E

D

(122)

If joists run at right angles to cornice, Illus. 123, measure 16" and test with a nail. If you locate solid wood, measure again at 16". When you locate joists, draw guide lines. Drill holes through A, Illus. 119, and screw cornice to joists.

When fastening a valance to basement walls, use expansion plugs or molly bolts, Illus. 124. Always buy size with screws that fit mounting plate on traverse track or fluorescent channel.

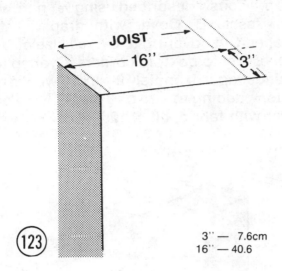

JOIST

16"

3"

3" — 7.6cm
16" — 40.6

(123)

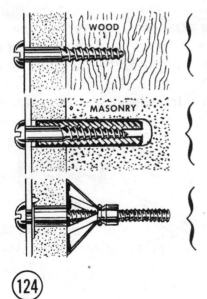

WOOD

MASONRY

(124)

Here are the various kinds of screws and fasteners that can be used.

When fastening through plaster, wall board or plywood into wall studs, use wood screws provided.

This expanding type fastener is usually used in brick or masonry walls.

It is first necessary to drill a hole. Your hardware dealer can provide the drill and plugs required.

This Screw-Anchor is used when fastening to a hollow wall. The wings on this fastener press firmly against wall covering when bolt or screw is fastened securely.

FABRIC COVERED VALANCE

Build valance as previously described using ⅛" hardboard or ¼" plywood for fascia B. Cover with drapery fabric or matching wallpaper. Cut covering to overall size of B and C, plus overage necessary to boxfold corners. Overlap top and turn front edge under approximately 2". If you want a padded valance, cut cotton padding to size of B plus C. Glue padding in position, cover with fabric, Illus. 125.

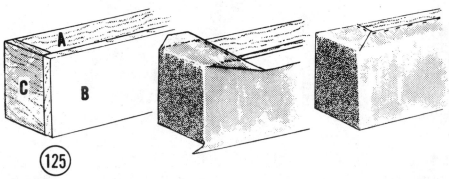

(125)

Illus. 126 shows another way of making a fabric covered valance. Cut A width required to position drapery track away from sill, by length to project beyond edge of casing. Cut C same width as A by 8, 10 to 12" in height. Cut 1 x 2 stiffener B to length required. Nail C to A, C to B. Cut fabric to size required. Cut a piece of buckram to overall size of valance. Staple buckram in position. Fold fabric over bottom edge of B, 2", over top and to inside edge of C. Glue, tack or staple.

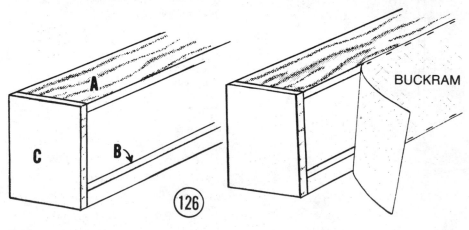

BUCKRAM

(126)

To build valance, Illus. 117, cut parts A, B, C, Illus. 127, from 1 x 6, 1 x 8, 1 x 10 or ½, ⅝ or ¾" plywood. For those who prefer a more graceful facing board, ⅜" plywood can be used for B.

A

B

C

(127)

Since the width of a valance is dependent on length and personal taste, play safe, revise the full size paper pattern before sawing lumber.

Using a square, draw a vertical center line. Working from center line, and with bottom edge of pattern lined up with bottom edge of lumber, trace pattern to overall length required, Illus. 128. If an extra few inches of length are required, it can be added to the straight part at both ends, or the curve at center can be stretched out. Creating a valance that enhances the decor of a room helps shape the hand of fate. Always alter the printed pattern to length and width your partner requests. Place pattern in position and get approval initialed in non-fading ink. Saw to shape. If you have a saber saw, you make like magic.

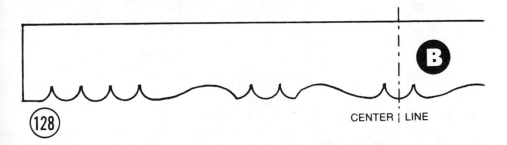

(128)

B

CENTER LINE

NOTE: Since facing board B, Illus. 127, projects over end of C, cut B to length required.

Using a square, draw lines to deepest point of scallop, Illus. 129. Make saw cuts, then each scallop.

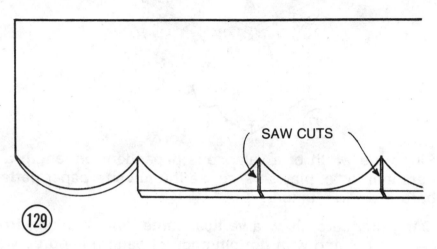

SAW CUTS

(129)

Cut end C, Illus. 130, to height of B and to width of A. Apply glue and brad C to A, B to A and C in position shown, Illus. 127, using 4 penny finishing nails.

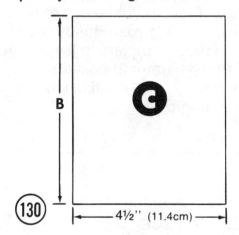

B

C

(130)

|← 4½" (11.4cm) →|

Valances can be fastened with angle irons as shown, Illus. 131, or nailed to casing, Illus. 132. Glue or nail wood trim to top edge, Illus. 133. Miter cut corners.

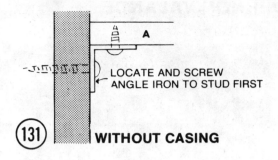

A

LOCATE AND SCREW
ANGLE IRON TO STUD FIRST

(131) **WITHOUT CASING**

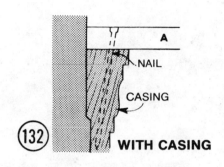

A

NAIL

CASING

(132) **WITH CASING**

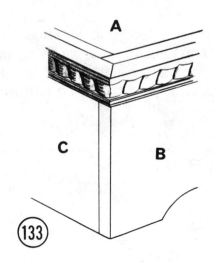

A

C

B

(133)

93

MOUNT VERNON VALANCE

Making the valance shown in Illus. 115 and 134 follows the same general procedure. Length of valance can be altered by extending straight run at both ends, or by spreading curve at center. For a really professional finish, miter cut carved wood trim, Illus. 118, 133. Glue and brad in position shown before fastening valance in position.

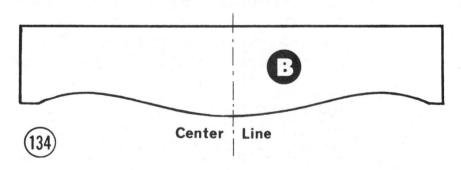

(134)   Center ¦ Line

THE CARVED WOOD VALANCE

(135)

This is one of the handsomest valances available, Illus. 135. The 3¼'' wide carved wood panel, Illus. 136, can be purchased in five foot lengths. Those interested in starting a part time business should build a sample and show it to the manager of every smart drapery shop. Offer to build on special order. The carving can be ordered from your building material retailer. If he doesn't handle same, write and we'll arrange shipment. Only apply carving across front as directions suggest.

(136)

The overall dimension of the valance, noted in Illus. 137, is suitable for glass curtains. Follow directions on page 86 to estimate size required for curtains, draperies and indirect lighting.

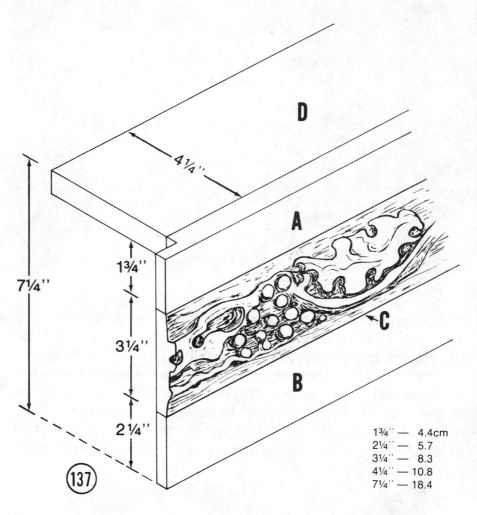

1¾" — 4.4cm
2¼" — 5.7
3¼" — 8.3
4¼" — 10.8
7¼" — 18.4

Illus. 138,139,140 show end view of parts A,B,C,D and E for a valance measuring 7¼'' high by 5'' deep.

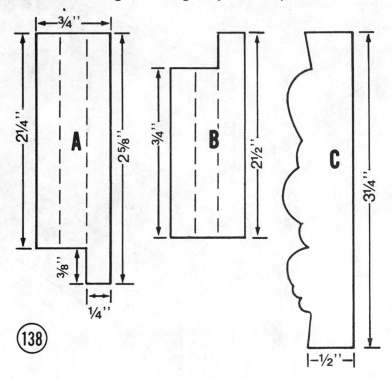

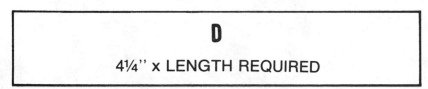

4¼'' x LENGTH REQUIRED

¼'' — 6.4mm	2¼'' — 5.7cm
3/8'' — 9.5	2½'' — 6.4
½'' — 12.7	2⅝'' — 6.7
¾'' — 19.0	3¼'' — 8.3
	4¼'' — 10.8

Those making valances or cornices for installation in a paneled room should glue ¼'' prefinished plywood to two pieces of ¼'' plywood.

Those using 1'' lumber for A and B should rabbet bottom edge of A and top of B to depth noted to receive edge of C.

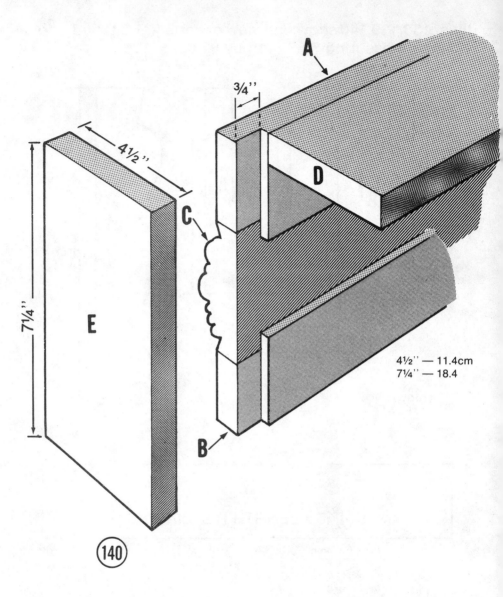

$4\frac{1}{2}$" — 11.4cm
$7\frac{1}{4}$" — 18.4

Rabbet ends of A and B ¾", or thickness of E, Illus. 140. Apply glue and insert C. Place in a jig until glue sets, Illus. 141.

Apply glue and nail A to D, E to D, A and B to E with 4 penny finishing nails. Countersink nail heads. Fill holes with putty.

Allow glue to set, then fasten track or rod to D. Screw 3 x 3" angle brackets to D, Illus. 142, in position casing on window or studs in wall require.

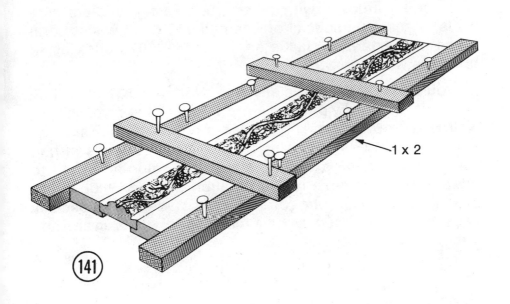

(141)

1 x 2

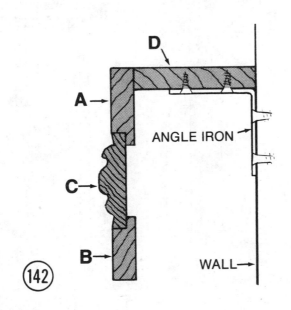

(142)

D

A→

ANGLE IRON

C→

B→

WALL→

99

HOW TO INSTALL TRAVERSE ROD
IN RECESSED WINDOWS

Recessed windows, with plaster, stone or concrete side walls, present no special problem. If you don't wish to drill holes in plaster for plastic anchors or molly bolts, fasten brackets with epoxy.

Or you can make a free standing "shadow box," Illus. 143, 144. Cut A and B width and length required to fit flush with wall. Use 1 x 6, 1 x 8 or ¾" plywood. Apply white glue and nail B to A with 6 penny finishing nails. Miter cut ends of half round rope molding to length required, glue and brad to edge. Fasten traverse rod in position desired. Slide entire box in position, hang drapery. This idea is especially satisfying in apartments where the "super" wants an arm and a leg to hang draperies.

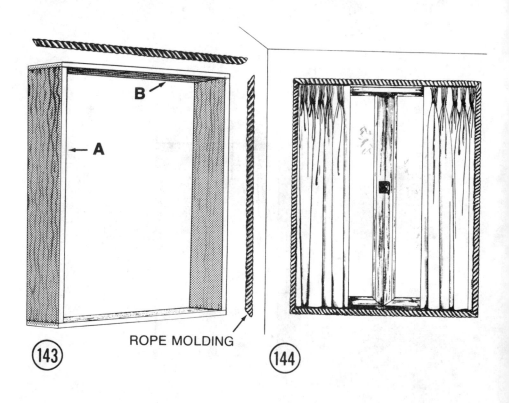

B

A

ROPE MOLDING

(143)   (144)

100

Use plastic expandable anchors, Illus. 145 and screws provided by manufacturer when fastening mounting plates to plaster walls, plasterboard, etc. If plaster is weak, or you plan on hanging heavy draperies, paint plastic anchor with epoxy before inserting. Allow glue to set prescribed period before hanging rod.

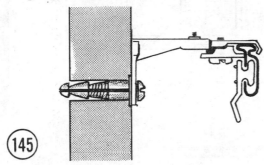

Illus. 146 shows another way of finishing a window wall in a wood paneled room. Remove ceiling trim within area to be covered, Illus. 147.

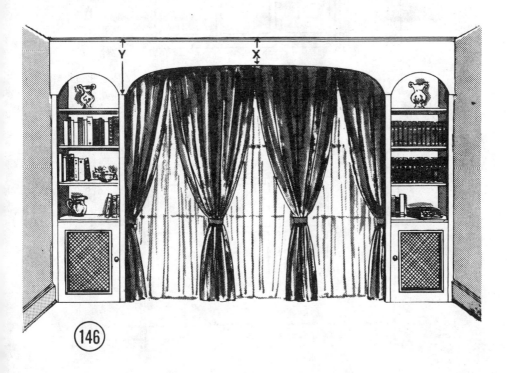

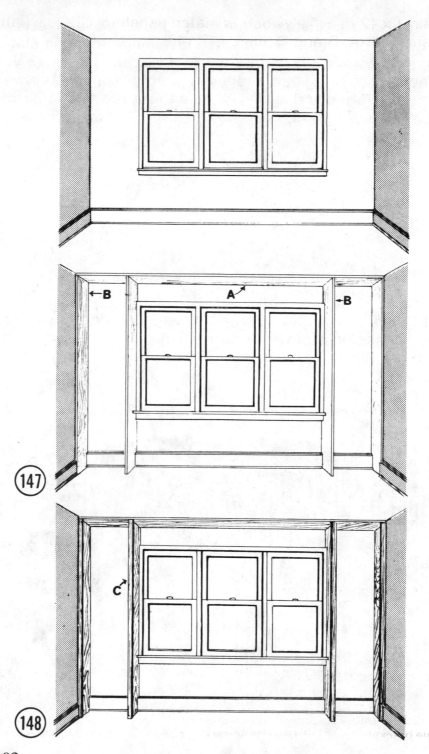

Stain 1 x 12 or ¾" plywood to match paneling. Cut to width desired for A, B and C, Illus. 147,148.

Cut A to length required and nail* in position to ceiling joists, or fasten in place following directions outlined on page 89. Cut B to length required. Notch B to fit sill and baseboard. Nail through B into casing using 6 penny finishing nails. Toenail to floor and to A.

Nail 1 x 2 C to edge of B, Illus. 148. Use ¼" paneling for fascia. Illus. 146 shows installation for a twelve foot wall, eight foot ceiling height.

Dimension X, Illus. 149, can be 12"; Y — 18 to 22". Glue and brad ¼" gusset plates to back of fascia when joining two pieces of plywood end to end. Space Z is optional. It can be 12 to 24". Measure Z, divide by 2. Use this as a radius for W.

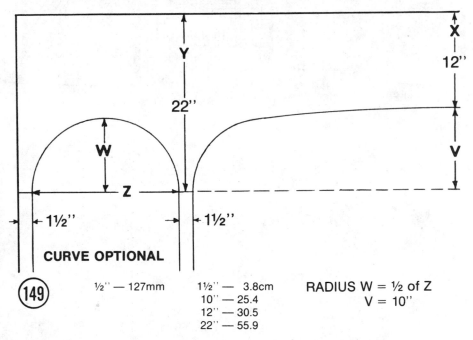

X

12"

Y

22"

W

V

Z

1½"   1½"

CURVE OPTIONAL

(149)   ½" — 127mm   1½" — 3.8cm   RADIUS W = ½ of Z
                        10" — 25.4   V = 10"
                        12" — 30.5
                        22" — 55.9

*Those installing valances, cornices, etc., in rental units are not allowed to permanently make any installation unless same is first approved by the landlord. Get approval in writing. Any permanent installation, those nailed, screwed or glued in place will become the property of the landlord. To make an installation without approval, one that can be removed, fasten B to A with angle brackets, Illus. 118. Use size screw that doesn't protrude through A or B.

Illus. 149 shows construction of door for cabinet. Cut ⅜"
flakeboard to size required. Drill 7/64" holes in position
indicated. Cut a piece of decorative fabric to size needed.
With good side facing out, staple fabric to flakeboard with
stapling gun. Miter cut molding to length needed. Apply glue
to miter and fasten in position with corner clamps. When glue
sets, fasten flakeboard to molding with ⅝" No. 5 screws.

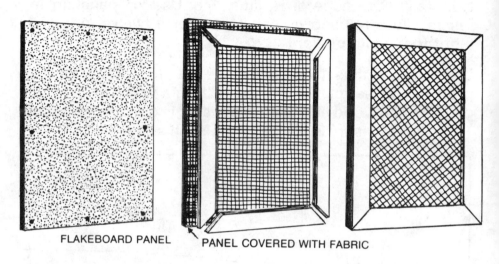

FLAKEBOARD PANEL   PANEL COVERED WITH FABRIC

(149)

FRAME A WINDOW

(150)

105

To frame a window, Illus. 150, or to build a wall shelf between two cabinets, Illus. 151; or a collector's display case, Illus. 152, 164, read following directions and note location of each part. For greater strength and rigidity, glue all permanent joints. Due to variance in lumber width and thickness, after you start to assemble, check size of additional parts against actual construction before cutting.

(151)

(152)

Since windows vary in size, measure X and Y, Illus. 153. Saw sill flush with side casing. Cut parts to fit.

Cut 1 x 4 top G, Illus. 154, to length of X.

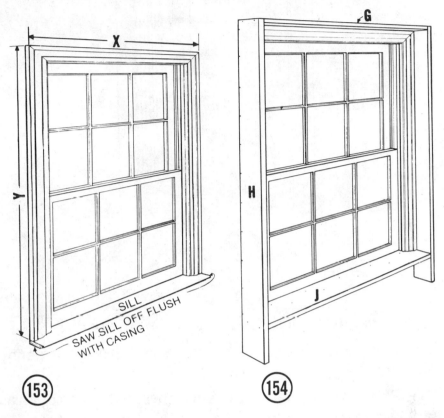

Cut two sides H to length of Y plus 5½''. Use 1 x 4. Glue and nail G in position with 6 penny finishing nails spaced about 8'' apart. Keep end of G flush with casing. Glue and nail H to casing and to G with 6 penny nails.

Cut sill J to length of X. Trace shape of casing on a pattern, then trace on J. Cut J with coping saw. Glue and nail J to sill; nail H to J with 6 penny nails.

Cut D and F slightly longer than length required. Pattern for D,E,F is printed on foldout. Draw a center line on D and F, Illus. 155. Tack D and F in position. Place E in position. Mark and cut D and F to exact length required. Nail in position following procedure previously outlined.

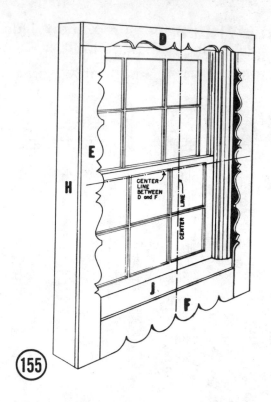

CENTER LINE BETWEEN D and F

CENTER LINE

G and H can be covered with matching plywood.

Glue and nail D to G and H; E to H and J using 4 penny finishing nails.

Cut F 5½'' wide by length required. Repeat pattern as often as needed.

Those who prefer a narrow frame around a window, Illus. 150, with or without shelves, can cut G and H from 1 x 2 or 1 x 3.

BUILD A WALL SHELF

This can be positioned between two cabinets, Illus. 151, or free standing, Illus. 152.

Cut two sides A — 1 x 6 x 27'', or to width and length desired, Illus. 156. Space shelves as indicated or at height preferred. Glue and brad ½ x 1⅜ x 5½'' stop molding B in position shown.

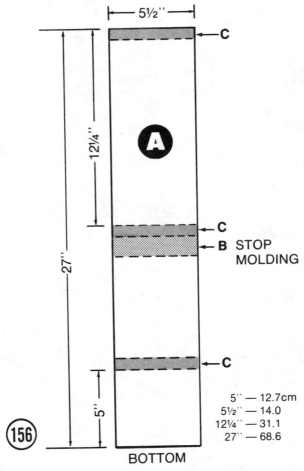

5'' — 12.7cm
5½'' — 14.0
12¼'' — 31.1
27'' — 68.6

BOTTOM

Cut three C, Illus. 157, to length required for 1 x 6. Glue and nail A to C with 6 penny nails.

Cut facing D, E and F to length required. Glue and brad in position, Illus. 158.

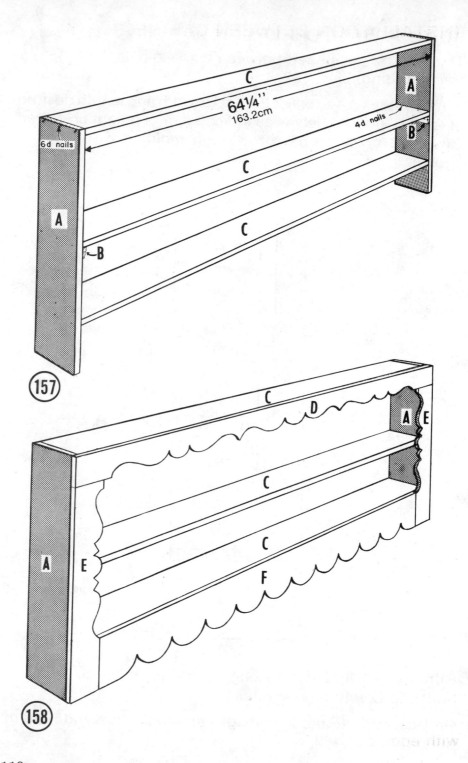

C

64¼"
163.2cm

A

6d nails

4d nails

B

A

B

C

C

(157)

C

D

A E

C

A

E

C

F

(158)

110

INSTALLATION BETWEEN CABINETS

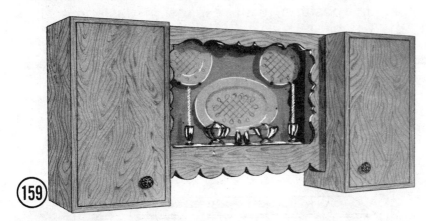

Nail ½ x 1⅜'' stop molding in position shown, Illus. 160, 22⅛'' from ceiling, or at height desired, with 8 penny nails. Check with level. Cut shelf L, Illus. 161, from ¾'' plywood or 1 x 8. Notch front corners to receive 1 x 2. Glue and nail L to K with 6 penny nails. Hold L level with 1 x 2 braces to floor.

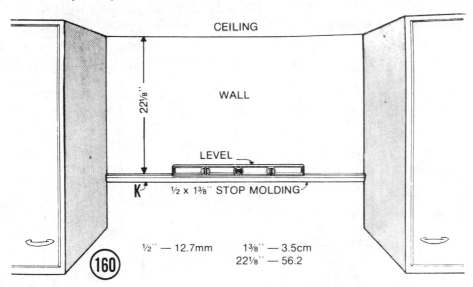

CEILING

WALL

22⅛''

LEVEL

K

½ x 1⅜'' STOP MOLDING

½'' — 12.7mm   1⅜'' — 3.5cm
                    22⅛'' — 56.2

Cut 1 x 2 ceiling cleat M to length required, Illus. 161. Notch ends of M to receive 1 x 2. Nail M flatwise to ceiling with 8 penny nails driven into ceiling joists. Keep edge of M in line with edge of L.

111

If ceiling joists run parallel to M and not in position where you can nail M to joists, drill holes through M and ceiling and fasten M in position with expansion fasteners, Illus. 161,122,123,124.

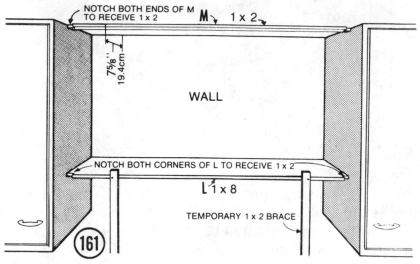

Cut two 1 x 2 side cleats N, Illus. 162, to length required. Glue and nail N to L and M with 4 penny finishing nails. Additional rigidity can be added by drilling holes through cabinet and fastening cabinet to N with 3 - 1¼'' No. 8 flathead screws.

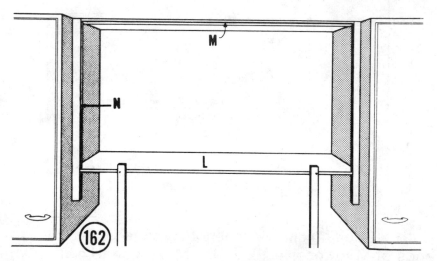

Cut facings D, E and F, Illus. 163, following directions previously outlined.

112

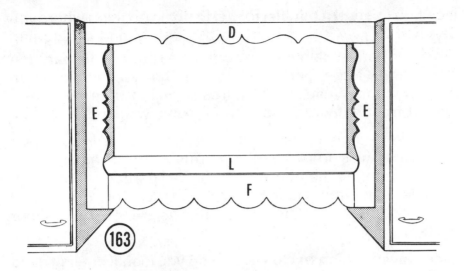

D

E   E

L

F

163

COLLECTORS' DISPLAY CASE

This case can be built using ⅛'' pegboard for a back. Cut G, H and L to width required to fit items to be displayed. If you want to use pegboard hooks, nail 1 x 2 to wall at top and bottom. Fasten cabinet to 1 x 2.

1 x 2 ——→

164

HOW TO BUILD A PARTITION

There are many major improvements you may wish to consider before paneling a room. One is to build a partition and divide a large room to make two. Or move location of an interior door. While this requires paneling both sides of a wall, it frequently provides more usable wall space.

When your house was built, certain interior walls were constructed as load bearing partitions. This means they support framing members, joists or wall partitions above. An outside wall frame is load bearing, and is customarily framed with a double 2 x 4 plate, and double header over each door and window.

Since any partition or closet framing you install doesn't need to be load bearing, only a single 2 x 4 plate is required, Illus. 165. Use a double 2 x 4 header over a door.

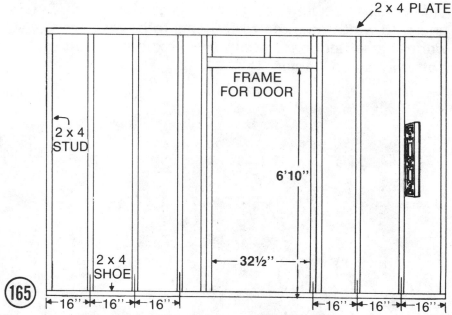

If new partition runs parallel to ceiling joists, try to position partition so it's directly under a joist. Joists in most houses built during the past 30 years were placed 16" on center. If you measure 16" from a wall, and every 16", you should locate a joist. Plate for partition can be spiked to joist with 16 penny nails.

114

If joists run parallel to new partition, and you can't conveniently locate the new partition under a joist, drill holes through 2 x 4 plate, and through ceiling. Fasten plate in position with expansion bolts, Illus. 59.

If joists run crosswise to new partition, partition can be placed wherever desired. Spike plate with 16 penny nails.

When drawing location for a partition on ceiling, always measure from same wall to both ends of the proposed partition, then snap a chalk line to indicate either the inside or outside edge of the 2 x 4 plate, Illus. 166. Before measuring a 2 x 4 for length, check end with a square, Illus. 167. Saw square, then measure and cut to length required.

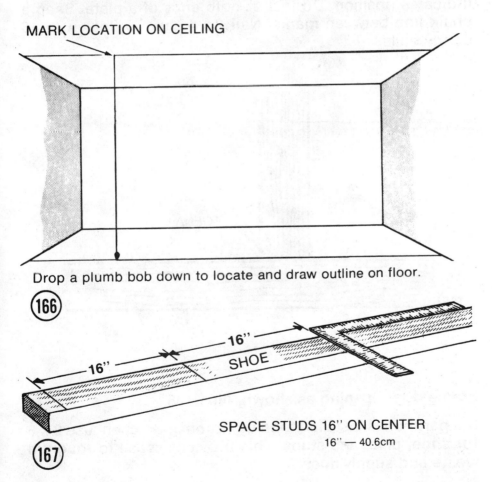

MARK LOCATION ON CEILING

Drop a plumb bob down to locate and draw outline on floor.

166

16"

16" SHOE

16"

167

SPACE STUDS 16" ON CENTER

16" — 40.6cm

115

Nail 2 x 4 plate to ceiling joists. If two lengths are required, cut ends square before cutting to length required.

Using a square, measure and draw lines across shoe every 16". Carefully measure distance between top of shoe and plate. Cut each stud to length required. Place in position. Use this stud to check length of other studs. Since most floors and ceilings are not exactly level, you will have to check length of each stud before cutting and nailing in position.

Using a level, check each stud in two directions before toenailing to shoe and plate. Use 8 penny nails, Illus. 168.

To position shoe directly under plate, drop a plumb bob down from side of plate, and mark floor where point of bob indicates position. Do this at both ends of a plate. Snap a chalk line between marks. Nail 2 x 4 shoe to floor with 16 penny nails.

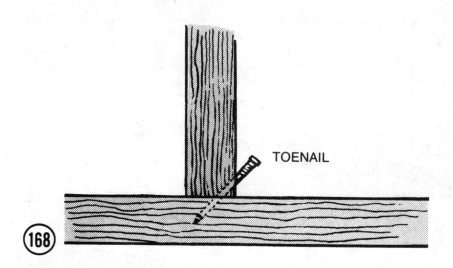

TOENAIL

168

Frame door opening as shown, Illus. 165.

If a partition is installed for a bathroom or kitchen, use 2 x 6 for shoe, plate and studs. This provides space to rough in waste and supply lines.

MODERNIZING
KITCHEN CABINETS, REFRIGERATOR

Old fashioned steel and wood cabinets, even a workable refrigerator can be given a new lease on life with prefinished paneling. Illus. 169 shows a before and after. A paneled refrigerator in a recreation room is real handy.

BEFORE

AFTER

To square up rounded edge and to cover door so it lines up with sides, cut 1 x 2 for A,B,C, Illus. 170. Cut a strip of plywood to overall size needed to cover A. Place a piece of plywood on highest plane of door. Adjust length of B so plywood on A and on door are on the same plane.

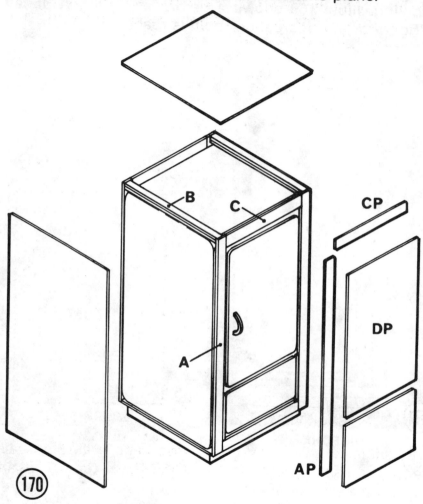

(170)

Apply waterproof glue to ends of B and nail A to B with 6 penny nails. Cut C to length required. Apply glue and toenail C to A. Allow ⅛" clearance on side without hinges, and clearance needed to allow door to open freely. Check frame with a square. Hold square with a 1 x 2 diagonal brace across A and B.

NOTE: Do not cover any grille. Always make a cutout where same is required.

You can fasten back frame to refrigerator, Illus. 171, with strips of perforated plumber's pipe strap. Remove screws in refrigerator to fasten strap in place. If refrigerator doesn't have screws in the right position, fasten additional 1 x 2 across back to secure frame.

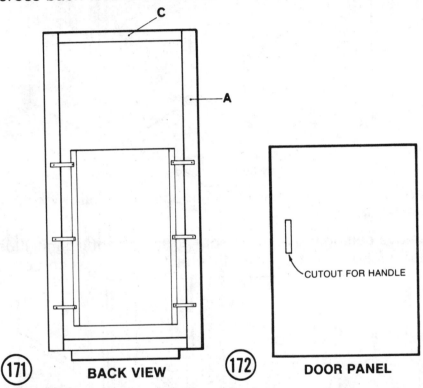

(171) **BACK VIEW**

(172) **DOOR PANEL**

CUTOUT FOR HANDLE

Cut panels to size required. Always keep grain vertically. Carefully measure ¼" panels AP, CP, DP, etc., Illus. 170, and cut each to size required.

Make cutout for handle, Illus. 172. Drill hole in position required and use a keyhole or saber saw. Sandpaper edges. Apply panel adhesive to 1 x 2 framing and fasten panels in position. Use epoxy or contact cement to bond panel to door. Most metal to wood cements recommend a ribbon around perimeter, daubs every 6, 8 to 10", Illus. 173. Finish exposed edge of paneling with Putty Stik.

119

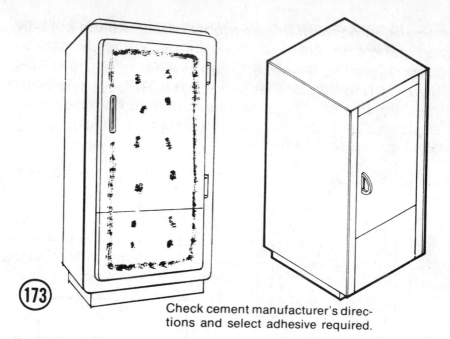

(173) Check cement manufacturer's directions and select adhesive required.

Steel and wood cabinets can be modernized following same general procedure.

Remove ceiling molding. Lay out cutting so soffit panel, Illus. 176, matches direction of grain, Illus. 174, on door, end, etc.

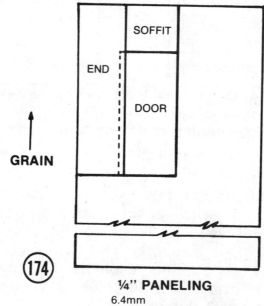

SOFFIT

END

DOOR

GRAIN

(174)

¼" PANELING
6.4mm

120

Hold parts in position or use rubber cement to temporarily fasten panels in place. If door binds, adjust hinges to accommodate the thicker door. If existing hinges can't be adjusted, test door with a continuous hinge or two 5" pieces, Illus. 175.

Cut end panel slightly oversize. Scribe to wall and cut to width required, Illus. 176.

Next cut strip A, Illus. 177, to width required. Apply to edge of door.

Use 1 x 2 or 5/4 x 2 to frame soffit to depth required so paneling finishes flush with door panel, Illus. 176. Cut end panel slightly oversize so you can scribe it to wall. After fitting to wall, cut to size required. Next cut a strip A for edge of door. If door has an exposed edge, Illus. 177. Or use a strip of paper thin matching wood tape on edge of door.

If you want to cover all edges of a wood door, remove hinges and trim door down to size required. Apply strips.

If you cut panels for wall cabinets ⅜" longer, top to bottom, than required, and allow the ⅜" to project beyond bottom edge, the projecting lip makes a good door pull. Or you can enhance cabinet by installing 1" dull brass door knobs.

If original hinge, or continuous hinge can't be used, apply 3½" colonial H-surface hinges, after applying panels.

Sand surface of steel cabinet before applying epoxy. Apply a 1 to 1½" strip of epoxy across bottom. This will insure extra strength when lip is used as a door pull.

Use waterproof glue when fastening plywood to wood. Panels can be held in position with blocks and clamps until glue bonds, Illus. 178.

Install a magnetic or roller door catch following manufacturer's directions, Illus. 179. Stain exposed edges. Use 3" strip of panel to finish soffit at ceiling, Illus. 36.

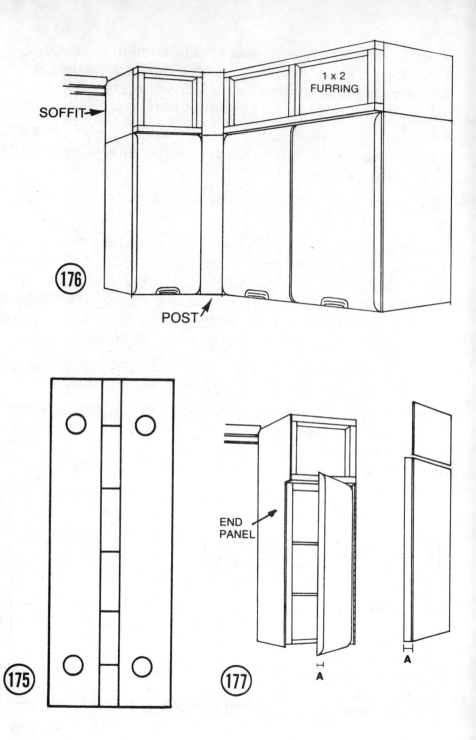

SOFFIT

1 x 2 FURRING

POST

⑦⑥

⑦⑤

END PANEL

⑦⑦

A

A

122

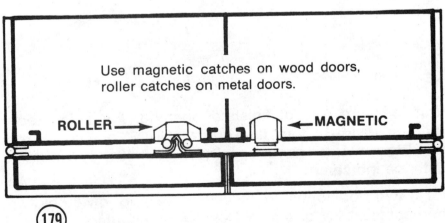

Use magnetic catches on wood doors, roller catches on metal doors.

ROLLER → ← MAGNETIC

BI-FOLDING DOOR HARDWARE

This hardware is available in kits containing all needed parts, Illus. 180. Always trim doors to fit hardware to opening following hardware manufacturer's directions. The hardware can be applied to four doors in 4'0'', 5'0'', 6'0'', 8'0'' openings. And to two doors in 2'0'', 2'6'' and 3'0'' openings. Doors may be 1⅛ or 1⅜'' thick and weigh up to 30 lbs. per door.

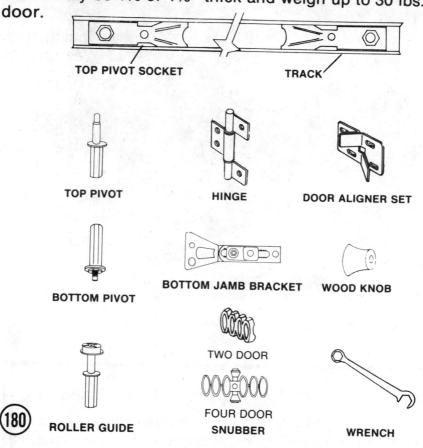

TOP PIVOT SOCKET   TRACK

TOP PIVOT   HINGE   DOOR ALIGNER SET

BOTTOM PIVOT   BOTTOM JAMB BRACKET   WOOD KNOB

TWO DOOR

FOUR DOOR

(180) ROLLER GUIDE   SNUBBER   WRENCH

First measure size of finished opening. For a four door opening, divide by four, then subtract 1/16'' or amount from each door manufacturer specifies, Illus. 181. Space doors distance indicated.

For a two door opening, measure opening, divide by two, then subtract ¼'' or amount hardware manufacturer specifies from width of each door.

124

EQUAL WIDTH DOORS
FOUR DOOR INSTALLATION

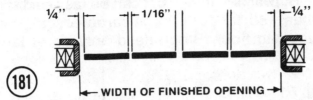

1/4" 1/16" 1/4"

WIDTH OF FINISHED OPENING

Check finished opening dimensions and trim doors to allow clearances shown.

To estimate height of doors, measure finished opening, Illus. 182, subtract 1⅞". This allows ⅝" minimum clearance at floor.

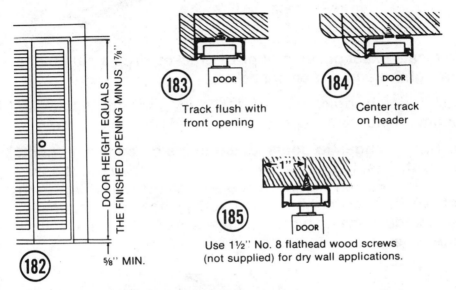

DOOR HEIGHT EQUALS
THE FINISHED OPENING MINUS 1⅞"

⅝" MIN.

Track flush with front opening

Center track on header

Use 1½" No. 8 flathead wood screws (not supplied) for dry wall applications.

Allow additional clearance at bottom for carpeting.

Track can be installed flush with edge of header, Illus. 183; centered, Illus. 184; or fastened to dry wall header, Illus. 185.

Cut track to length needed. Fasten to header with 1¼" screws, Illus. 186.

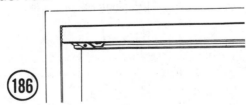

Check header with level. Shim track if necessary to level.

The bottom pivot bracket, Illus. 187, can be fastened to jamb and to floor, Illus. 188. If floor is to be carpeted, nail ½ or ¾" block of plywood to floor. Block need only be as large as bracket.

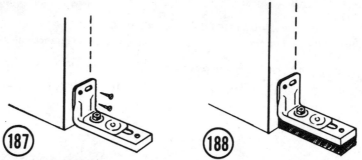

To locate exact position of pivot bracket, drop a plumb line through hole in top pivot socket.

Fasten jamb bracket, Illus. 187, in position. Allow ⅝" minimum clearance between floor and bottom of door.

To fasten hinges to doors, place doors on edge with good face out, Illus. 189. Use a piece of ½" plywood to space doors ½" apart. Fasten hinges 10" down from top, 10" up from bottom. Fasten third hinge in middle with screws supplied. Keep trade name on hinge up unless manufacturer specifies otherwise.

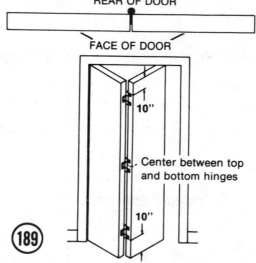

REAR OF DOOR

FACE OF DOOR

10"

Center between top and bottom hinges

10"

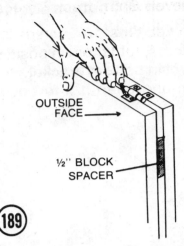

OUTSIDE FACE →

½" BLOCK SPACER

(189)

Drill 7/16" hole in center, Illus. 190, 1¼" from edge of door A, 1½" deep for top pivot. Drill same size hole in exact position in bottom of door A for bottom pivot.

Drill 7/16" hole in center, ⅞" from edge of door B, 1½" deep for guide roller, Illus. 190. Do not drill holes larger than 7/16".

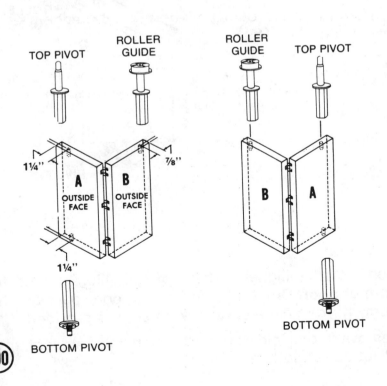

TOP PIVOT

ROLLER GUIDE

ROLLER GUIDE

TOP PIVOT

1¼"

⅞"

A

B

OUTSIDE FACE

OUTSIDE FACE

B

A

1¼"

BOTTOM PIVOT

BOTTOM PIVOT

(190)

Using a hammer, drive top and bottom pivots in door A; drive roller guide in door B, Illus. 191.

To install bi-folding doors, fold them in position shown, Illus. 191. Insert bottom pivot in bottom bracket. Slide top pivot up ramp into top socket and snap it into position with roller guide in track.

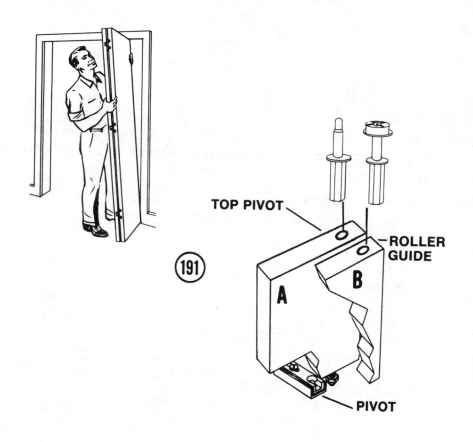

TOP PIVOT

ROLLER GUIDE

(191)

A   B

PIVOT

Fasten two door aligners to back of door, Illus. 192, 12" from bottom of door. Drill holes and fasten door pulls 36" from bottom, 1" from edge of door with screws provided.

To remove doors, fold in open position, raise straight up and lift pivot out at bottom.

128

Doors can be adjusted horizontally by loosening A on jamb bracket, Illus. 192, and at top socket B.

To raise doors, use wrench on bottom pivot at C, Illus. 192.

Snap one way self-centering snubber, Illus. 192, in center of track in a four door opening. Use a small snubber in a two door opening.

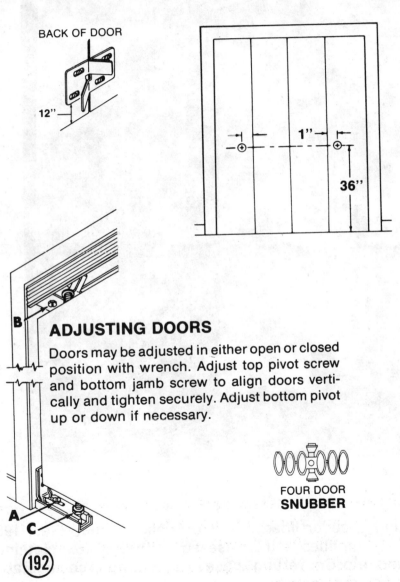

BACK OF DOOR

12"

1"

36"

ADJUSTING DOORS

Doors may be adjusted in either open or closed position with wrench. Adjust top pivot screw and bottom jamb screw to align doors vertically and tighten securely. Adjust bottom pivot up or down if necessary.

FOUR DOOR
SNUBBER

B

A
C

192

HOW TO BUILD A CEDAR ROOM

(193)

Building a cedar lined closet or walk-in room, Illus. 193, greatly simplifies out of season storage for clothing, blankets, etc. Converting space in an attic adds considerably to the value of your home.

Estimate amount of space you need and mark nearest rafter with an X, Illus. 194. Let's assume rafter X is ten feet from gable end. Drop a plumb bob down from outside face of rafter, and snap a chalk line across floor.

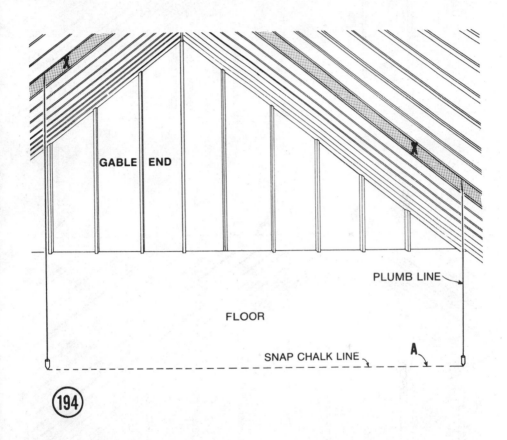

GABLE END

PLUMB LINE

FLOOR

SNAP CHALK LINE

A

(194)

Cut a 2 x 4 x 4'. Use it as a measuring pole B, Illus. 195. Plumb B in position (straight in two directions) under X. Keep face of B flush with outside face of X. Snap chalk lines C on floor, D on rafters. C and D now indicate framing.

While an 8 x 10' room offers ample storage space, draw line E, Illus. 196, wherever space permits. Measure 8'0'' from line C and snap line E. Using a plumb bob, mark and snap chalk line F. Lines A, C and E now indicate area of cedar room.

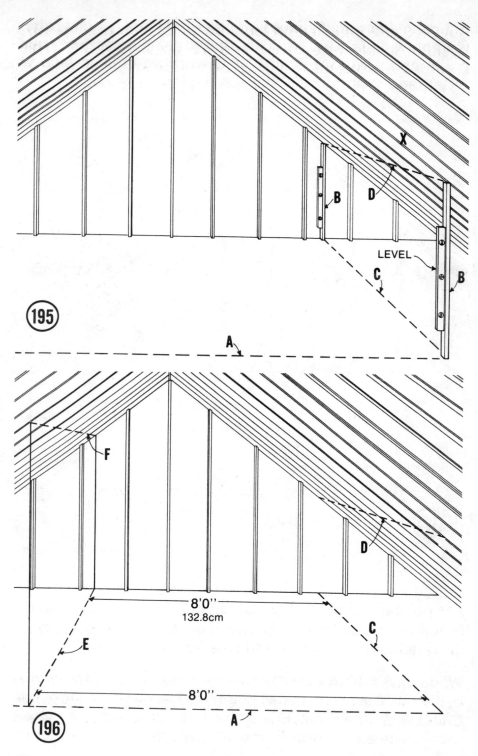

(195)

X

B

D

LEVEL

C

B

A

(196)

F

D

8'0"
132.8cm

E

C

8'0"

A

132

Cut 2 x 3 or 2 x 4 to length required for G1 and G2, Illus. 197. Position inside face of G1 and G2 on lines A,C,E. This permits nailing studs P, Illus. 208, to outside face of rafter X. Toenail G1 and G2 to floor joists with 16 penny nails.

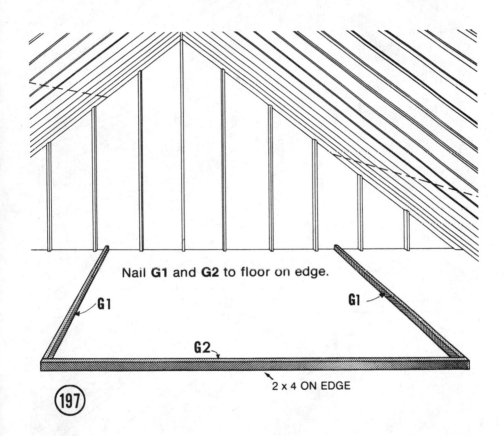

Nail **G1** and **G2** to floor on edge.

G1

G1

G2

(197)

2 x 4 ON EDGE

Cut two 2 x 4 for headers H, Illus. 198.

With inside edge of H on line D, tack H temporarily in place, Illus. 199. Keep end of H flush with outside face of X.

Using a square, draw location of each rafter on H. Remove H and make sawcuts to depth pitch of rafter requires, Illus. 199, 200. Chisel notch in H. Using 16 penny nails, nail H to rafters with inside edge of H on line D, Illus. 198.

133

Cut 2 x 4 studs J, Illus. 198, to length required. Toenail J to G1 and to H, directly under each rafter, with 8 penny nails.

Nail 2 x 4 stud K, Illus. 198, 201, in position shown. K provides a nailor for inside corner of cedar lining.

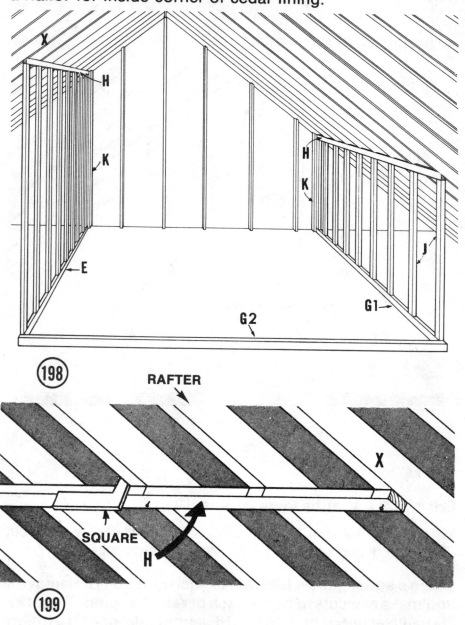

Frame wall E to H following same procedure, Illus. 198.

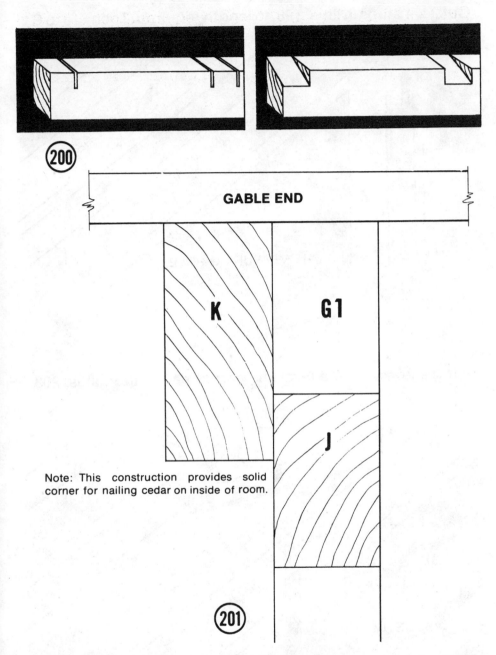

200

GABLE END

K

G1

J

Note: This construction provides solid corner for nailing cedar on inside of room.

201

To determine position of ceiling joists, cut a 2 x 4 x 7'1". Place against gable rafter, Illus. 202. Check with level to make certain it's plumb. Draw line on gable rafter and on X. Snap a chalk line across rafters.

135

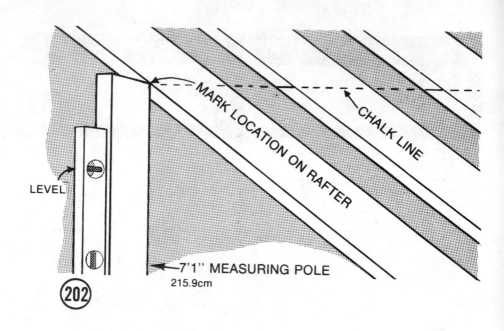

MARK LOCATION ON RAFTER

CHALK LINE

LEVEL

7'1" MEASURING POLE
215.9cm

202

Using a level, draw a level line across each rafter, Illus. 203.

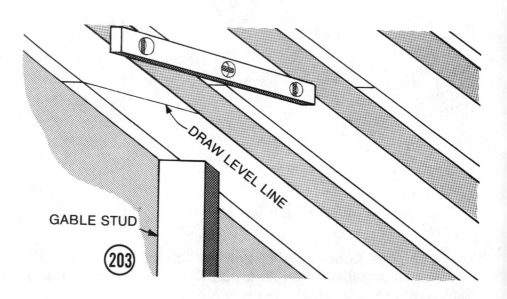

DRAW LEVEL LINE

GABLE STUD

203

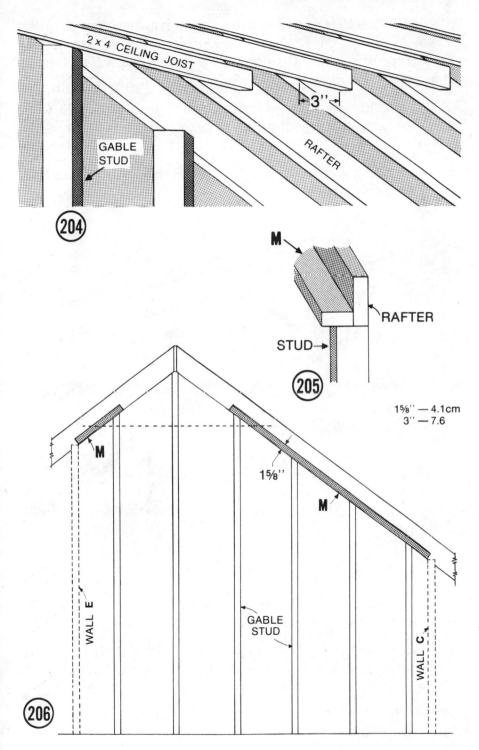

2 × 4 CEILING JOIST

3"

GABLE
STUD

RAFTER

(204)

M

RAFTER

STUD

(205)

1⅝'' — 4.1cm
3'' — 7.6

M

1⅝''

M

WALL E

GABLE
STUD

WALL C

(206)

137

Cut 2 x 4 joists to length required so each extends over rafter at least 3", Illus. 204. Check each with level and nail to rafters using 10 penny nails. Do not nail a joist between rafters at gable end. Nail joist to inside face of rafters X.

Cut 2 x 4 nailors M. Toenail M to gable rafters, Illus. 205, 206, flush with bottom edge of rafter. M provides a nailor for cedar ceiling boards.

Saw ends of 2 x 4 joist N, Illus. 207, to pitch of roof. Spike N to M and to gable studs.

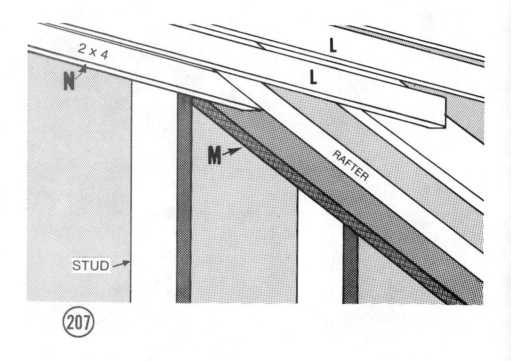

(207)

Cut 2 x 4 studs P, Illus. 208, to length needed. Plumb with level and nail in position shown to rafter, toenail to G2.

Illus. 208 shows rough opening for a 2'8" x 6'0" door. Stud opening to allow space for size of door selected. Cut G2 off at door opening.

Cut 2 x 4 nailors Q, Illus. 209, to angle and length required. Allow Q to project 1" below edge of X.

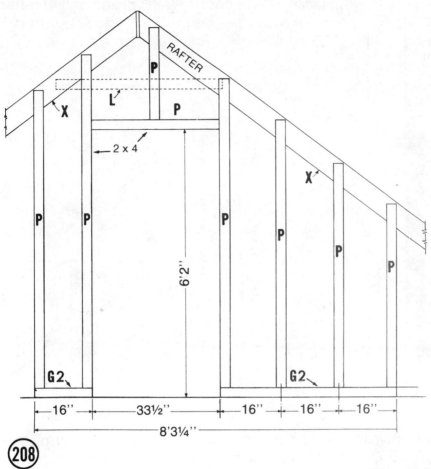

RAFTER

P

L

X

P

2 x 4

P   P

P

X'

6'2"

P

P

P

G2

G2

|—16"—|——33½"——|—16"—|—16"—|—16"—|

|————————8'3¼"————————|

(208)

16" — 40.6cm
17¾" — 45.0
33½" — 85.1
6'2" — 188.0
8'3¼" — 252.1

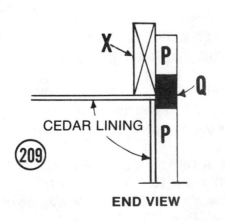

X

P

Q

CEDAR LINING

(209)

P

END VIEW

139

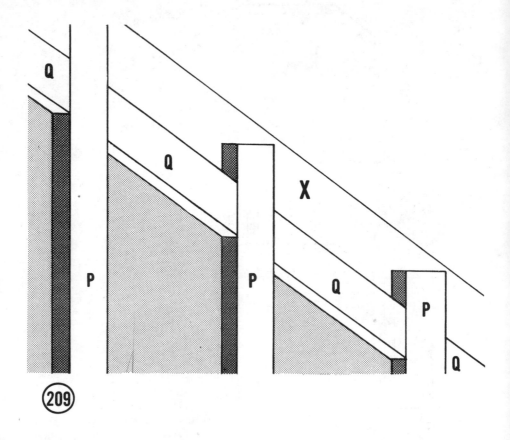

(209)

Run BX or non-metallic cable for overhead lighting, Illus. 210. Book #694 Electrical Repairs Simplified provides complete details.

Staple #15 felt horizontally to studs enclosing room. Allow each course to overlap at least 2".

Sheath interior walls with ⅜" cedar closet lining. Quality cedar comes packaged in random lengths. It comes with a tongue and grooved edge and end.

Apply cedar lining in direction arrows indicate in Illus. 210, 211. Start at C and work to F. Use 4 penny finishing nails. Then start at E and work to F. Bevel plane edge of cedar when you come to a break in ceiling.

140

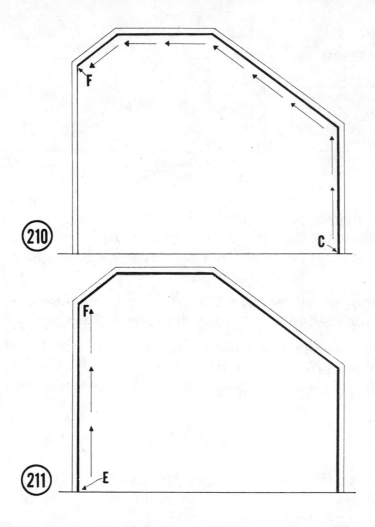

Sheath gable end, starting at floor and working up. Next sheath wall with door opening, starting at floor. Saw ends of cedar flush with door opening.

Lay #15 felt over floor area and nail cedar flooring parallel with gable end. Use 8 penny cut nails. Run flooring through door opening and bevel outside edge. This bevel makes it easier to roll clothes racks into the room.

Sheath outside walls of room with ¼" paneling. Nail paneling to studs with 6 penny finishing nails.

Run trim around door opening, Illus. 212.

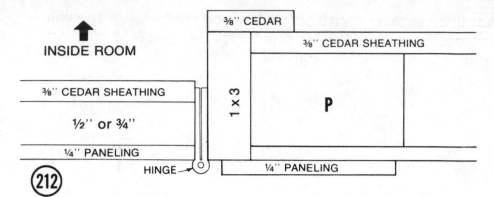

INSIDE ROOM

⅜" CEDAR

⅜" CEDAR SHEATHING

⅜" CEDAR SHEATHING

1 x 3

P

½" or ¾"

¼" PANELING

¼" PANELING

HINGE

(212)

Cut ½" flakeboard for door to size of opening, or build a frame, Illus. 66. Glue or nail ¼" paneling to outside face (¾" wire brads can be used). Nail ⅜" cedar sheathing to inside face.

Hang door with three 2½ x 2½" loose pin butt hinges. Install a door lock set following manufacturer's directions.

If shelves are desired, build same along 4 ft. wall following dimensions given in Illus. 213.

¼" — 6.4mm
⅜" — 9.5
½" — 12.7
¾" — 19.0

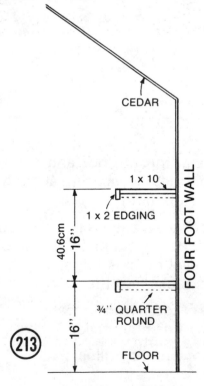

CEDAR

1 x 10

1 x 2 EDGING

40.6cm

16"

FOUR FOOT WALL

¾" QUARTER ROUND

16"

(213)

FLOOR

Apply cedar over 1 x 10 or ½" plywood shelves. Cut shelves to length required. Nail ¾" quarter round to walls in position shelf requires. Toenail shelves in place. Nail 1 x 2 center post in position, then nail 1 x 2 shelf stiffeners in place, Illus. 214.

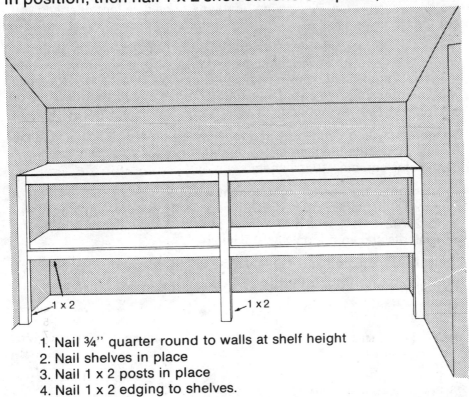

1 x 2   1 x 2

1. Nail ¾" quarter round to walls at shelf height
2. Nail shelves in place
3. Nail 1 x 2 posts in place
4. Nail 1 x 2 edging to shelves.

(214)   SHOWING SHELVES AT 4'0" WALL (OPTIONAL)

To obtain maximum protection, your cedar room should be constructed as airtight as possible, even to the point of weatherstripping the door to keep full strength of aroma.

Seal all inside corners of room at floor, walls and ceiling with ¾" quarter round molding. Nail molding with 4 penny finishing nails.

DO NOT APPLY ANY FINISH TO THE FACE OF CEDAR.

If building a room against gable end of attic interferes with a ventilating louver or window, room can be built away from gable end by framing a fourth wall. Follow directions for wall A, but do not frame for a door.

HOW TO THINK METRIC

Government officials concerned with the adoption of the metric system are quick to warn anyone from attempting to make precise conversions. One quickly accepts this advice when they begin to convert yards to meters or vice versa. Place a metric ruler alongside a foot ruler and you get the message fast.

Since a meter equals 1.09361 yards, or 39⅜"+, the decimals can drive you up a creek. The government men suggest accepting a rough, rather than exact equivalent. They recommend considering a meter in the same way you presently use a yard. A kilometer as 0.6 of a mile. A kilogram or kilo as just over two pounds. A liter, a quart, with a small extra swig.

To more fully appreciate why a rough conversion is preferable, note the 6" rule alongside the metric rule. A meter contains 100 centimeters. A centimeter contains 10 millimeters.

As an introduction to the metric system, we used a metric rule to measure standard U.S. building materials. Since a 1 x 2 measures anywhere from ¾ to 25/32 x 1½", which is typical of U.S. lumber sizes, the metric equivalents shown are only approximate.

Consider 1" equal to 2.54 centimeters; 10" = 25.4cm.

To multiply 4¼" into centimeters: 4.25 × 2.54 = 10.795 or 10.8cm.

INCH	—	MILLIMETER
1"		25.4
15/16		23.8
7/8		22.2
13/16		20.6
3/4		19.0
11/16		17.5
5/8		15.9
9/16		14.3
1/2		12.7
7/16		11.1
3/8		9.5
5/16		7.9
1/4		6.4
3/16		4.8
1/8		3.2
1/16		1.6

INCHES		—	CENTIMETERS
1			2.54
	1/8		2.9
		1/4	3.2
	3/8		3.5
		1/2	3.8
	5/8		4.1
		3/4	4.4
	7/8		4.8
2			5.1
	1/8		5.4
		1/4	5.7
	3/8		6.0
		1/2	6.4
	5/8		6.7
		3/4	7.0
	7/8		7.3
3			7.6
	1/8		7.9
		1/4	8.3
	3/8		8.6
		1/2	8.9
	5/8		9.2
		3/4	9.5
	7/8		9.8

4			10.2
	1/8		10.5
		1/4	10.8
	3/8		11.1
		1/2	11.4
	5/8		11.7
		3/4	12.1
	7/8		12.4
5			12.7
	1/8		13.0
		1/4	13.3
	3/8		13.7
		1/2	14.0
	5/8		14.3
		3/4	14.6
	7/8		14.9
6			15.2
	1/8		15.6
		1/4	15.9
	3/8		16.2
		1/2	16.5
	5/8		16.8
		3/4	17.1
	7/8		17.5
7			17.8
	1/8		18.1
		1/4	18.4
	3/8		18.7
		1/2	19.1
	5/8		19.4
		3/4	19.7
	7/8		20.0
8			20.3
	1/8		20.6
		1/4	21.0
	3/8		21.3
		1/2	21.6
	5/8		21.9
		3/4	22.2
	7/8		22.5
9			22.9
	1/8		23.2
		1/4	23.5
	3/8		23.8
		1/2	24.1
	5/8		24.4
		3/4	24.8
	7/8		25.1
10			25.4
	1/8		25.7
		1/4	26.0
	3/8		26.4
		1/2	26.7
	5/8		27.0
		3/4	27.3
	7/8		27.6

11			27.9
	1/8		28.3
		1/4	28.6
	3/8		28.9
		1/2	29.2
	5/8		29.5
		3/4	29.8
	7/8		30.2
12			30.5
	1/8		30.8
		1/4	31.1
	3/8		31.4
		1/2	31.8
	5/8		32.1
		3/4	32.4
	7/8		32.7
14			35.6
16			40.6
20			50.8
30			76.2
40			101.6
50			127.0
60			152.4
70			177.8
80			203.2
90			228.6
100			254.0

FEET = INCHES = CENTIMETERS

FEET		INCHES		CENTIMETERS
1	=	12	=	30.5
2	=	24	=	61.0
3	=	36	=	91.4
4	=	48	=	121.9
5	=	60	–	152.4
6	=	72	=	182.9
7	=	84	=	213.4
8	=	96	=	243.8
9	=	108	=	274.3
10	=	120	=	304.8
11	=	132	=	335.3
12	=	144	=	365.8
13	=	156	=	396.2
14	=	168	=	426.7
15	=	180	=	457.2
16	=	192	=	487.7
17	=	204	=	518.2
18	=	216	=	548.6
19	=	228	=	579.1
20	=	240	=	609.6

HANDY - REFERENCE - LUMBER
PLYWOOD - FLAKEBOARD - HARDBOARD - MOLDINGS

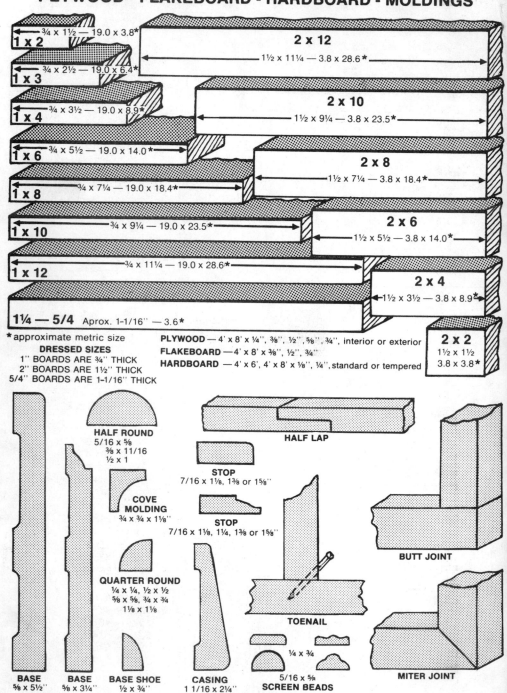

1 x 2 — ¾ x 1½ — 19.0 x 3.8*

1 x 3 — ¾ x 2½ — 19.0 x 6.4*

1 x 4 — ¾ x 3½ — 19.0 x 8.9*

1 x 6 — ¾ x 5½ — 19.0 x 14.0*

1 x 8 — ¾ x 7¼ — 19.0 x 18.4*

1 x 10 — ¾ x 9¼ — 19.0 x 23.5*

1 x 12 — ¾ x 11¼ — 19.0 x 28.6*

1¼ — 5/4   Aprox. 1-1/16'' — 3.6*

2 x 12 — 1½ x 11¼ — 3.8 x 28.6*

2 x 10 — 1½ x 9¼ — 3.8 x 23.5*

2 x 8 — 1½ x 7¼ — 3.8 x 18.4*

2 x 6 — 1½ x 5½ — 3.8 x 14.0*

2 x 4 — 1½ x 3½ — 3.8 x 8.9*

2 x 2 — 1½ x 1½ — 3.8 x 3.8*

* approximate metric size

DRESSED SIZES
1'' BOARDS ARE ¾'' THICK
2'' BOARDS ARE 1½'' THICK
5/4'' BOARDS ARE 1-1/16'' THICK

PLYWOOD — 4' x 8' x ¼'', ⅜'', ½'', ⅝'', ¾'', interior or exterior
FLAKEBOARD — 4' x 8' x ⅜'', ½'', ¾''
HARDBOARD — 4' x 6', 4' x 8' x ⅛'', ¼'', standard or tempered

HALF ROUND
5/16 x ⅝
⅜ x 11/16
½ x 1

COVE MOLDING
¾ x ¾ x 1⅛''

QUARTER ROUND
¼ x ¼, ½ x ½
⅝ x ⅝, ¾ x ¾
1⅛ x 1⅛

STOP
7/16 x 1⅛, 1⅜ or 1⅝''

STOP
7/16 x 1⅛, 1¼, 1⅜ or 1⅝''

TOENAIL

SCREEN BEADS
¼ x ¾
5/16 x ⅝

HALF LAP

BUTT JOINT

MITER JOINT

BASE
⅝ x 5½''

BASE
⅝ x 3¼''

BASE SHOE
½ x ¾''

CASING
1 1/16 x 2¼''